AMALGAMATED INTERNATIONAL & U.S. INLAND NAVIGATION RULES

Below is an amalgamation of the International Regulations for Preventing Collisions at Sea and the U.S. Inland Navigation Rules, their Annexes, and associated Federal regulations. Unlike its hard-copy predecessors--the *U.S. Coast Guard's Navigation Rules: International-Inland (Commandant Instruction 16672.2 series)* and *Navigation Rules and Regulations Handbook* ISBN:9780160954061, GPO Stock Number: 050-012-00519-2—it foregoes side-by-side portrayal and adopts a single-page layout that sets out the differences between each set of Rules. It is also considerably smaller in size; thus quicker to view online, download, and, print.

We strive to ensure its accuracy; nonetheless, we make no claims or guarantees of such and expressly disclaim liability for its use. Corrections, comments, or suggestions are welcomed by cgnav@uscg.mil.

An up to date printed or downloaded* copy of this Amalgamation, or the Navigation Rules as published in the United States Coast Pilot® (which also includes embedded graphics) may be used to meet the 'copy of these Rules' requirement of Inland Rule 1(g). For our policy on the use of electronic publications and charts, *see Navigation and Vessel Inspection Circular *(NVIC) 01-16 CH-2*.

Click on:

- blue-text to jump to a definition or provision in U.S. Code (U.S.C.) or the Code of Federal Regulations (CFR).
- 📷 to view a graphic rendition of a Rule.
- ↖ to return to the beginning of the Table of Contents.

Legend:

1. Provisions unique to either Rule are denoted by respectively titled double border frames, i.e. Rules 1(a-e), 9(e), 24(g)(ii), 34(a-b), 38(a-d), Annex I, 2(c), and, Annex III,1(g);

2. Text unique to either Rule is denoted by angle brackets; International Rules text is ‹ single-bracketed › and Inland Rules text is ‹‹ *double-bracketed* ›› and italicized;

3. Instances such as "…§§83.xx in / with / of…this section / subpart / part of this Rule, etc." are redacted with the enumerated Rule(s) or section number, e.g. Rule 18(e) states: "...with the Rules of this Part" or "...with the Rules of this Subpart (Rules 4-19) (§§83.04 through 83.19)" is redacted as "...with Rules 4-19";

4. Instances such as "paragraph (x)", "section (y)", subsection (1)(z), etc. are redacted with a section symbol, i.e. §(x), §(y) or §(1)(z);

5. Dissimilar paragraph or section numbering are redacted and separated by a dagger symbol, i.e. §(b)‡(ii);

6. Implementing or Interpretative Rules (33 CFR 81-90) are denoted by a single border frame immediately following the Rule they implement or interpret; and,

7. Annotated text added by the U.S. Coast Guard is denoted by {curly brackets}.

TABLE OF CONTENTS

II - Conduct of Vessels in Sight of One Another

III - Conduct of Vessels in Restricted Visibility

PART C - LIGHTS AND SHAPES

PART D - SOUND AND LIGHT SIGNALS

PART E - EXEMPTIONS

PART F - VERIFICATION OF COMPLIANCE WITH THE PROVISIONS OF THE CONVENTION {COLREGS only}

ANNEXES

OTHER ASSOCIATED REFERENCES

NAVIGATION RULES

PART A - GENERAL

Rule 1 - Application 🕇

International	Inland
(a) These Rules shall apply to all vessels upon the high seas and in all waters connected therewith navigable by seagoing vessels.	(a) These rules apply to all vessels upon the *inland waters of the United States, and to vessels of the United States on the Canadian waters of the* Great Lakes *to the extent that there is no conflict with Canadian law. These Rules have preemptive effect over State or local regulation within the same field.*
(b) Nothing in these Rules shall interfere with the operation of special rules made by an appropriate authority for roadsteads, harbors, rivers, lakes, or inland waterways connected with the high seas and navigable by seagoing vessels. Such special rules shall conform as closely as possible to these Rules.	(b)(i)*These rules constitute special rules made by an appropriate authority within the meaning of Rule 1(b) of the International Regulations for Preventing Collisions at Sea, 1972, including annexes currently in force for the United States ("International Regulations").* *(ii) All vessels complying with the construction and equipment requirements of the International Regulations are considered to be in compliance with these Rules.*
(c) Nothing in these Rules shall interfere with the operation of any special rules made by the Government of any State with respect to additional station or signal lights, shapes or whistle signals for ships of war and vessels proceeding under convoy, or with respect to additional station or signal lights or shapes for fishing vessels engaged in fishing as a fleet. These additional stations or signal lights, shapes or whistle signals shall, so far as possible, be such that they cannot be mistaken for any light, shape, or signal authorized elsewhere under these Rules.	(c) Nothing in these Rules shall interfere with the operation of any special rules made by the *Secretary of the Navy* with respect to additional station or signal lights and shapes or whistle signals for ships of war and vessels proceeding under convoy, or *by the Secretary* with respect to additional station or signal lights and shapes for fishing vessels engaged in fishing as a fleet. These additional station or signal lights and shapes or whistle signals shall, so far as possible, be such that they cannot be mistaken for any light, shape or signal authorized elsewhere under these Rules. *Notice of such special rules shall be published in the Federal Register and, after the effective date specified in such notice, they shall have effect as if they were a part of these Rules.*
(d) Traffic separation schemes may be adopted by the Organization for the purpose of these Rules.	(d) Traffic separation schemes may be *established* for the purposes of these Rules. *Vessel traffic service regulations may be in effect in certain areas.*
(e) Whenever the Government concerned shall have determined that a vessel of special construction or purpose cannot comply fully with the provisions of any of these Rules with respect to number, position, range or arc of visibility of lights or shapes, as well as to the disposition and characteristics of sound-signaling appliances, such vessel shall comply with such other provisions in regard to number, position, range or arc of visibility of lights or shapes, as well as to the disposition and characteristics of sound-signaling appliances, as the Government shall have determined to be the closest possible compliance with these Rules in respect to that vessel.	(e) Whenever the *Secretary* determines that a vessel or class of vessels of special construction or purpose cannot comply fully with the provisions of any of these Rules with respect to the number, position, range, or arc of visibility of lights or shapes, as well as to the disposition and characteristics of sound-signaling appliances, *the* vessel shall comply with such other provisions in regard to the number, position, range, or arc of visibility of lights or shapes, as well as to the disposition and characteristics of sound-signaling appliances, as the *Secretary* shall have determined to be the closest possible compliance with these Rules. *The Secretary may issue a certificate of* alternative compliance *for a vessel or class of vessels specifying the closest possible compliance with these Rules. The Secretary of the Navy shall make these determinations and issue certificates of* alternative compliance for vessels of the Navy.

Inland

(f) The Secretary may accept a certificate of alternative compliance *issued by a contracting party to the International*

Regulations if it determines that the alternative compliance standards of the contracting party are substantially the same as those of the United States.

(g) The operator of each self-propelled vessel 12 meters or more in length shall carry, on board and maintain for ready reference, a copy of these Rules.

{An up to date printed or downloaded* copy of this Amalgamation, or the Navigation Rules as published in the United States Coast Pilot® (which also includes embedded graphics) may be used to meet the 'copy of these Rules' requirement of Inland Rule 1(g). For our policy on the use of electronic publications and charts, *see Navigation and Vessel Inspection Circular (NVIC) 01-16 CH-2.}

Rule 2 - Responsibility ᵗ

(a) Nothing in these Rules shall exonerate any vessel, or the owner, master, or crew thereof, from the consequences of any neglect to comply with these Rules or of the neglect of any precaution which may be required by the ordinary practice of seamen, or by the special circumstances of the case.

(b) In construing and complying with these Rules due regard shall be had to all dangers of navigation and collision and to any special circumstances, including the limitations of the vessels involved, which may make a departure from these Rules necessary to avoid immediate danger.

Rule 3 - General Definitions ᵗ

For the purpose of these Rules, except where the context otherwise requires:

(a) The word "vessel" includes every description of watercraft, including non-displacement craft, WIG craft, and seaplanes, used or capable of being used as a means of transportation on water.

(b) The term "power-driven vessel" means any vessel propelled by machinery.

(c) The term "sailing vessel" means any vessel under sail provided that propelling machinery, if fitted, is not being used.

(d) The term "vessel engaged in fishing" means any vessel fishing with nets, lines, trawls, or other fishing apparatus which restrict maneuverability, but does not include a vessel fishing with trolling lines or other fishing apparatus which do not restrict maneuverability.

(e) The term "seaplane" includes any aircraft designed to maneuver on the water.

(f) The term "vessel not under command" means a vessel which through some exceptional circumstance is unable to maneuver as required by these Rules and is therefore unable to keep out of the way of another vessel.

(g) The term "vessel restricted in her ability to maneuver" means a vessel which from the nature of her work is restricted in her ability to maneuver as required by these Rules and is therefore unable to keep out of the way of another vessel. The term "vessels restricted in their ability to maneuver" shall include but not be limited to:

    (i) A vessel engaged in laying, servicing, or picking up a navigational mark, submarine cable or pipeline;
    (ii) A vessel engaged in dredging, surveying or underwater operations;
    (iii) A vessel engaged in replenishment or transferring persons, provisions or cargo while underway;
    (iv) A vessel engaged in the launching or recovery of aircraft;
    (v) A vessel engaged in mine clearance operations;
    (vi) A vessel engaged in a towing operation such as severely restricts the towing vessel and her tow in their ability to deviate from their course.

International

(h) The term "vessel constrained by her draft" means a power-driven vessel which because of her draft in relation to the available depth and width of navigable water is severely restricted in her ability to deviate from the course she is following.

(i) The word "underway" means that a vessel is not at anchor, or made fast to the shore, or aground.

(j) The words "length" and "breadth" of a vessel mean her length overall and greatest breadth.

(k) Vessels shall be deemed to be in sight of one another only when one can be observed visually from the other.

(l) The term "restricted visibility" means any condition in which visibility is restricted by fog, mist, falling snow, heavy rainstorms, sandstorms, or any other similar causes.

(m) The term "Wing-In-Ground (WIG)" craft means a multimodal craft which, in its main operational mode, flies in close proximity to the surface by utilizing surface-effect action.

Inland

(n) "Western Rivers" means the Mississippi River, its tributaries, South Pass, and Southwest Pass, to the navigational demarcation lines {30 CFR 80} dividing the high seas from harbors, rivers and other inland waters of the United States, and the Port Allen-Morgan City Alternate Route, and that part of the Atchafalaya River above its junction with the Port Allen-Morgan City Alternate Route including the Old River and the Red River.

(o) "Great Lakes" means the Great Lakes and their connecting tributary waters including the Calumet River as far as the Thomas J. O'Brien Lock and Controlling Waters (between mile 326 and 327), the Chicago River as far as the east side of the Ashland Avenue Bridge (between mile 321 and 322), and the Saint Lawrence River as far east as the lower exit of Saint Lambert Lock.

(p) "Secretary" means the Secretary of the Department in which the Coast Guard is operating.

(q) "Inland Waters" means the navigable waters of the United States shoreward of the navigational demarcation lines {30 CFR 80} dividing the high seas from harbors, rivers and other inland waters of the United States and the waters of the Great Lakes on the United States side of the International Boundary.

(r) Inland Rules or Rules means these Inland Navigational Rules and the annexes thereto, which govern the conduct of vessels and specify the lights, shapes, and sound signals that apply on inland waters.

(s) International Regulations means the International Regulations for Preventing Collisions at Sea, 1972, including annexes currently in force for the United States.

Implementing Rule (33 CFR 89.25) **Waters upon which Inland Rules 9(a)(ii), 14(d), and 15(b) apply**.

Inland Rules 9(a)(ii), 14(d), and 15(b) apply to "Waters specified by the Secretary / defined in 33 CFR 89.25", means the Great Lakes, Western Rivers, and the following specified waters: (a) Tennessee-Tombigbee Waterway, (b) Tombigbee River, (c) Black Warrior River, (d) Alabama River, (e) Coosa River, (f) Mobile River above the Cochrane Bridge at St Louis Point, (g) Flint River, (h) Chattahoochee River, and, (i) the Apalachicola River above its confluence with the Jackson River.

PART B - STEERING AND SAILING RULES

I - Conduct of Vessels in Any Condition of Visibility.

Rule 4 - Application 🔼

Rules 4 - 10 apply in any condition of visibility.

Rule 5 - Lookout 🔼

Every vessel shall at all times maintain a proper look-out by sight and hearing as well as by all available means appropriate in the prevailing circumstances and conditions so as to make a full appraisal of the situation and of the risk of collision.

Rule 6 - Safe Speed 🔼

Every vessel shall at all times proceed at a safe speed so that she can take proper and effective action to avoid collision and be stopped within a distance appropriate to the prevailing circumstances and conditions. In determining a safe speed the following factors shall be among those taken into account:

(a) By all vessels:

      (i) The state of visibility;
      (ii) The traffic density including concentrations of fishing vessels or any other vessels;
      (iii) The maneuverability of the vessel with special reference to stopping distance and turning ability in the prevailing conditions;
      (iv) At night, the presence of background light such as from shore lights or from back scatter from her own lights;
      (v) The state of wind, sea and current, and the proximity of navigational hazards;
      (vi) The draft in relation to the available depth of water.

(b) Additionally, by vessels with operational radar:

    (i) The characteristics, efficiency and limitations of the radar equipment;
    (ii) Any constraints imposed by the radar range scale in use;
    (iii) The effect on radar detection of the sea state, weather and other sources of interference;
    (iv) The possibility that small vessels, ice and other floating objects may not be detected by radar at an adequate range;
    (v) The number, location and movement of vessels detected by radar;
    (vi) The more exact assessment of the visibility that may be possible when radar is used to determine the range of vessels or other objects in the vicinity.

Rule 7 - Risk of Collision 🡑

(a) Every vessel shall use all available means appropriate to the prevailing circumstances and conditions to determine if risk of collision exists. If there is any doubt such risk shall be deemed to exist.

(b) Proper use shall be made of radar equipment if fitted and operational, including long-range scanning to obtain early warning of risk of collision and radar plotting or equivalent systematic observation of detected objects.

(c) Assumptions shall not be made on the basis of scanty information, especially scanty radar information.

(d) In determining if risk of collision exists the following considerations shall be among those taken into account:

    (i) Such risk shall be deemed to exist if the compass bearing of an approaching vessel does not appreciably change.
    (ii) Such risk may sometimes exist even when an appreciable bearing change is evident, particularly when approaching a very large vessel or a tow or when approaching a vessel at close range.

Rule 8 - Action to Avoid Collision 🡑

(a) Any action taken to avoid collision shall be taken in accordance with Rules 4-19 and shall if the circumstances of the case admit, be positive, made in ample time and with due regard to the observance of good seamanship.

(b) Any alteration of course and/or speed to avoid collision shall, if the circumstances of the case admit, be large enough to be readily apparent to another vessel observing visually or by radar; a succession of small alterations of course and/or speed should be avoided.

(c) If there is sufficient sea room, alteration of course alone may be the most effective action to avoid a close-quarters situation provided that it is made in good time, is substantial and does not result in another close-quarters situation.

(d) Action taken to avoid collision with another vessel shall be such as to result in passing at a safe distance. The effectiveness of the action shall be carefully checked until the other vessel is finally past and clear.

(e) If necessary to avoid collision or allow more time to assess the situation, a vessel shall slacken her speed or take all way off by stopping or reversing her means of propulsion.

(f)(i) A vessel which, by any of these Rules, is required not to impede the passage or safe passage of another vessel shall, when required by the circumstances of the case, take early action to allow sufficient sea room for the safe passage of the other vessel.

    (ii) A vessel required not to impede the passage or safe passage of another vessel is not relieved of this obligation if approaching the other vessel so as to involve risk of collision and shall, when taking action, have full regard to the action which may be required by Rules 4-19.

    (iii) A vessel, the passage of which is not to be impeded remains fully obliged to comply with Rules 4-19 when the two vessels are approaching one another so as to involve risk of collision.

Rule 9 - Narrow Channels 🡑

(a) ‹‹(i)›› A vessel proceeding along the course of a narrow channel or fairway shall keep as near to the outer limit of the channel or fairway which lies on her starboard side as is safe and practicable.

Inland

(ii) Notwithstanding Rule 9(a)(i) and Rule 14(a), a power-driven vessel operating in narrow channel or fairway on the Great Lakes, Western Rivers, or waters specified by the Secretary, and proceeding downbound with a following current shall have the right-of-way over an upbound vessel, shall propose the manner and place of passage, and shall initiate the maneuvering signals prescribed by Rule 34(a)(i), as appropriate. The vessel proceeding upbound against the current shall hold as necessary to permit safe passing.

(b) A vessel of less than 20 meters in length or a sailing vessel shall not impede the passage of a vessel ‹ which › ‹‹ *that* ›› can safely navigate only within a narrow channel or fairway.

(c) A vessel engaged in fishing shall not impede the passage of any other vessel navigating within a narrow channel or fairway.

(d) A vessel ‹ shall › ‹‹ *must* ›› not cross a narrow channel or fairway if such crossing impedes the passage of a vessel which can safely navigate only within that channel or fairway. The latter vessel ‹ may › ‹‹ *must* ›› use the signal prescribed in Rule 34(d) if in doubt as to the intention of the crossing vessel.

International	Inland
(e)(i) In a narrow channel or fairway when overtaking can take place only if the vessel to be overtaken has to take action to permit safe passing, the vessel intending to overtake shall indicate her intention by sounding the appropriate signal prescribed in Rule 34(c)(ii). The vessel to be overtaken shall, if in agreement, sound the appropriate signal prescribed in Rule 34(c)(i) and take steps to permit safe passing. If in doubt she may sound the signals prescribed in Rule 34(d).	(e)(i) In a narrow channel or fairway when overtaking, *the power-driven vessel intending to overtake another power-driven vessel* shall indicate her intention by sounding the appropriate signal prescribed in Rule 34(c) *and take steps to permit safe passing. The power-driven vessel being overtaken, if in agreement, shall sound the same signal and may, if specifically agreed to,* take steps to permit safe passing. If in doubt she shall sound the signal prescribed in Rule 34(d).

(e)(ii) This rule does not relieve the overtaking vessel of her obligation under Rule 13.

(f) A vessel nearing a bend or an area of a narrow channel or fairway where other vessels may be obscured by an intervening obstruction shall navigate with particular alertness and caution and shall sound the appropriate signal prescribed in Rule 34(e).

(g) Any vessel shall, if the circumstances of the case admit, avoid anchoring in a narrow channel.

Rule 10 - Traffic Separation Schemes 🔔

(a) This Rule applies to traffic separation schemes ‹ adopted by the Organization › and does not relieve any vessel of her obligation under any other rule.

(b) A vessel using a traffic separation scheme shall:

(i) Proceed in the appropriate traffic lane in the general direction of traffic flow for that lane.
(ii) So far as is practicable keep clear of a traffic separation line or separation zone.
(iii) Normally join or leave a traffic lane at the termination of the lane, but when joining or leaving from either side shall do so at as small an angle to the general direction of traffic flow as practicable.

(c) A vessel, shall so far as practicable, avoid crossing traffic lanes but if obliged to do so shall cross on a heading as nearly as practicable at right angles to the general direction of traffic flow.

(d)(i) A vessel shall not use an inshore traffic zone when she can safely use the appropriate traffic lane within the adjacent traffic separation scheme. However, vessels of less than 20 meters in length, sailing vessels and vessels engaged in fishing may use the inshore traffic zone.

(ii) Notwithstanding Rule 10(d)(i), a vessel may use an inshore traffic zone when en route to or from a port, offshore installation or structure, pilot station or any other place situated within the inshore traffic zone, or to avoid immediate danger.

(e) A vessel, other than a crossing vessel or a vessel joining or leaving a lane shall not normally enter a separation zone or cross a separation line except:

(i) in cases of emergency to avoid immediate danger;
(ii) to engage in fishing within a separation zone.

(f) A vessel navigating in areas near the terminations of traffic separation schemes shall do so with particular caution.

(g) A vessel shall so far as practicable avoid anchoring in a traffic separation scheme or in areas near its terminations.

(h) A vessel not using a traffic separating scheme shall avoid it by as wide a margin as is practicable.

(i) A vessel engaged in fishing shall not impede the passage of any vessel following a traffic lane.

(j) A vessel of less than 20 meters in length or a sailing vessel shall not impede the safe passage of a power-driven vessel following a traffic lane.

(k) A vessel restricted in her ability to maneuver when engaged in an operation for the maintenance of safety of navigation in a traffic separation scheme is exempted from complying with this Rule to the extent necessary to carry out the operation.

(l) A vessel restricted in her ability to maneuver when engaged in an operation for the laying, servicing or picking up of a submarine cable, within a traffic separation scheme, is exempted from complying with this Rule to the extent necessary to carry out the operation.

II - Conduct of Vessels in Sight of One Another

Rule 11 - Application ⚓

Rules 11-18 apply to vessels in sight of one another.

Rule 12 - Sailing Vessels ⚓

(a) When two sailing vessels are approaching one another, so as to involve risk of collision, one of them shall keep out of the way of the other as follows:

> (i) when each has the wind on a different side, the vessel which has the wind on the port side shall keep out of the way of the other;
> (ii) when both have the wind on the same side, the vessel which is to windward shall keep out of the way of the vessel which is to leeward;
> (iii) if a vessel with the wind on the port side sees a vessel to windward and cannot determine with certainty whether the other vessel has the wind on the port or on the starboard side, she shall keep out of the way of the other.

(b) For the purposes of this Rule, the windward side shall be deemed to be the side opposite that on which the mainsail is carried or, in the case of a square-rigged vessel, the side opposite to that on which the largest fore-and-aft sail is carried.

Rule 13 - Overtaking ⚓

(a) Notwithstanding anything contained in the Rules 4-18, any vessel overtaking any other shall keep out of the way of the vessel being overtaken.

(b) A vessel shall be deemed to be overtaking when coming up with a another vessel from a direction more than 22.5 degrees abaft her beam, that is, in such a position with reference to the vessel she is overtaking, that at night she would be able to see only the sternlight of that vessel but neither of her sidelights.

(c) When a vessel is in any doubt as to whether she is overtaking another, she shall assume that this is the case and act accordingly.

(d) Any subsequent alteration of the bearing between the two vessels shall not make the overtaking vessel a crossing vessel within the meaning of these Rules or relieve her of the duty of keeping clear of the overtaken vessel until she is finally past and clear.

Rule 14 - Head-on Situation ⚓

(a) ‹‹ Unless otherwise agreed ›› when two power-driven vessels are meeting on reciprocal or nearly reciprocal courses so as to involve risk of collision each shall alter her course to starboard so that each shall pass on the port side of the other.

(b) Such a situation shall be deemed to exist when a vessel sees the other ahead or nearly ahead and by night she could see the masthead lights of the other in a line or nearly in a line and/or both sidelights and by day she observes the corresponding aspect of the other vessel.

(c) When a vessel is in any doubt as to whether such a situation exists she shall assume that it does exist and act accordingly.

Inland
(d) Notwithstanding Rule 14(a), a power-driven vessel operating on the Great Lakes, Western Rivers, or waters specified by the Secretary, and proceeding downbound with a following current shall have the right-of-way over an upbound vessel, shall propose the manner of passage, and shall initiate the maneuvering signals prescribed by Rule 34(a)(i), as appropriate.

Rule 15 - Crossing Situation ⚓

(a) When two power-driven vessels are crossing so as to involve risk of collision, the vessel which has the other on her own starboard side shall keep out of the way and shall, if the circumstances of the case admit, avoid crossing ahead of the other vessel.

Inland
(b) Notwithstanding Rule 15(a), on the Great Lakes, Western Rivers, or water specified by the Secretary, a power-driven

vessel crossing a river shall keep out of the way of a power-driven vessel ascending or descending the river.

Rule 16 - Action by Give-way Vessel 🔝

Every vessel which is directed to keep out of the way of another vessel shall, so far as possible, take early and substantial action to keep well clear.

Rule 17- Action by Stand-on Vessel 🔝

(a)(i) Where one of two vessels is to keep out of the way, the other shall keep her course and speed.

(ii) The latter vessel may, however, take action to avoid collision by her maneuver alone, as soon as it becomes apparent to her that the vessel required to keep out of the way is not taking appropriate action in compliance with these Rules.

(b) When, from any cause, the vessel required to keep her course and speed finds herself so close that collision cannot be avoided by the action of the give-way vessel alone, she shall take such action as will best aid to avoid collision.

(c) A power-driven vessel which takes action in a crossing situation in accordance with Rule 17(a)(ii) to avoid collision with another power-driven vessel shall, if the circumstances of the case admit, not alter course to port for a vessel on her own port side.

(d) This Rule does not relieve the give-way vessel of her obligation to keep out of the way.

Rule 18 - Responsibilities Between Vessels 🔝

Except where Rules 9, 10, and 13 otherwise require:

(a) A power-driven vessel underway shall keep out of the way of:

(i) a vessel not under command;
(ii) a vessel restricted in her ability to maneuver;
(iii) a vessel engaged in fishing;
(iv) a sailing vessel.

(b) A sailing vessel underway shall keep out of the way of:

(i) a vessel not under command;
(ii) a vessel restricted in her ability to maneuver;
(iii) a vessel engaged in fishing.

(c) A vessel engaged in fishing when underway shall, so far as possible, keep out of the way of:

(i) a vessel not under command;
(ii) a vessel restricted in her ability to maneuver.

International

(d)(i) Any vessel other than a vessel not under command or a vessel restricted in her ability to maneuver shall, if the circumstances of the case admit, avoid impeding the safe passage of a vessel constrained by her draft, exhibiting the signals in Rule 28.

(ii) A vessel constrained by her draft shall navigate with particular caution having full regard to her special condition.

(e) A seaplane on the water shall, in general, keep well clear of all vessels and avoid impeding their navigation. In circumstances, however, where risk of collision exists, she shall comply with Rules 4-19.

(f)(i) A WIG craft shall, when taking off, landing and in flight near the surface, keep well clear of all other vessels and avoid impeding their navigation;

(ii) a WIG craft operating on the water surface shall comply with Rules 4-19 as a power-driven vessel.

III - Conduct of Vessels in Restricted Visibility

Rule 19 - Conduct of Vessels in Restricted Visibility 🔝

(a) This Rule applies to vessels not in sight of one another when navigating in or near an area of restricted visibility.

(b) Every vessel shall proceed at a safe speed adapted to the prevailing circumstances and conditions of restricted visibility. A power-driven vessel shall have her engines ready for immediate maneuver.

(c) Every vessel shall have due regard to the prevailing circumstances and conditions of restricted visibility when complying with Rules 4-10.

(d) A vessel which detects by radar alone the presence of another vessel shall determine if a close-quarters situation is developing and/or risk of collision exists. If so, she shall take avoiding action in ample time, provided that when such action consists of an alteration in course, so far as possible the following shall be avoided:

      (i) An alteration of course to port for a vessel forward of the beam, other than for a vessel being overtaken;
      (ii) An alteration of course toward a vessel abeam or abaft the beam.

(e) Except where it has been determined that a risk of collision does not exist, every vessel which hears apparently forward of her beam the fog signal of another vessel, or which cannot avoid a close-quarters situation with another vessel forward of her beam, shall reduce her speed to be the minimum at which she can be kept on her course. She shall if necessary take all her way off and in any event navigate with extreme caution until danger of collision is over.

PART C - LIGHTS AND SHAPES

Rule 20 - Application 🕭

(a) Rules 20-31 shall be complied with in all weathers.

(b) The Rules concerning lights shall be complied with from sunset to sunrise, and during such times no other lights shall be exhibited, except such lights which cannot be mistaken for the lights specified in these Rules or do not impair their visibility or distinctive character, or interfere with the keeping of a proper look-out.

(c) The lights prescribed by these Rules shall, if carried, also be exhibited from sunrise to sunset in restricted visibility and may be exhibited in all other circumstances when it is deemed necessary.

(d) The Rules concerning shapes shall be complied with by day.

(e) The lights and shapes specified in these Rules shall comply with the provisions of Annex I of these Rules.

Inland
(f) A vessel's navigation lights and shapes may be lowered if necessary to pass under a bridge.

Rule 21 - Definitions 🖻 🕭

(a) "Masthead light" means a white light placed over the fore and aft centerline of the vessel showing an unbroken light over an arc of the horizon of 225 degrees and so fixed as to show the light from right ahead to 22.5 degrees abaft the beam on either side of the vessel ‹‹ *except that on a vessel of less than 12 meters in length the masthead light shall be placed as nearly as practicable to the fore and aft centerline of the vessel* ››.

(b) "Sidelights" means a green light on the starboard side and a red light on the port side each showing an unbroken light over an arc of the horizon of 112.5 degrees and so fixed as to show the light from right ahead to 22.5 degrees abaft the beam on its respective side. In a vessel of less than 20 meters in length the sidelights may be combined in one lantern carried on the fore and aft centerline of the vessel ‹‹ , *except that on a vessel of less than 12 meters in length the sidelights when combined in one lantern shall be placed as nearly as practicable to the fore and aft centerline of the vessel* ››.

(c) "Sternlight" means a white light placed as nearly as practicable at the stern showing an unbroken light over an arc of the horizon of 135 degrees and so fixed as to show the light 67.5 degrees from right aft on each side of the vessel.

(d) "Towing light" means a yellow light having the same characteristics as the "sternlight" defined in Rule 21(c).

(e) "All-round light" means a light showing an unbroken light over an arc of the horizon of 360 degrees.

(f) "Flashing light" means a light flashing at regular intervals at a frequency of 120 flashes or more per minute.

Inland
(g) "Special flashing light" means a yellow light flashing at regular intervals at a frequency of 50 to 70 flashes per minute, placed as far forward and as nearly as practicable on the fore and aft centerline of the tow and showing an unbroken light over

an arc of the horizon of not less than 180 degrees nor more than 225 degrees and so fixed as to show the light from right ahead to abeam and no more than 22.5 degrees abaft the beam on either side of the vessel.

ANNEX V – Pilot Rules {Inland Only}

Law Enforcement Vessels { Flashing blue light } (33 CFR 88.05)

(a) Law enforcement vessels may display a flashing blue light when engaged in direct law enforcement or public safety activities. This light must be located so that it does not interfere with the visibility of the vessel's navigation lights.

(b) The blue light described in this section may be displayed by law enforcement vessels of the United States and the States and their political subdivisions.

Public Safety Vessels { Alternating flashing red and yellow light } (33 CFR 88.07)

(a) Vessels engaged in government sanctioned public safety activities, and commercial vessels performing similar functions, may display an alternately flashing red and yellow light signal. This identification light signal must be located so that it does not interfere with the visibility of the vessel's navigation lights. The identification light signal may be used only as an identification signal and conveys no special privilege. Vessels using the identification light signal during public safety activities must abide by the inland navigation rules, and must not presume that the light or the exigency gives them precedence or right of way.

(b) Public safety activities include but are not limited to patrolling marine parades, regattas, or special water celebrations; traffic control; salvage; firefighting; medical assistance; assisting disabled vessels; and search and rescue.

Rule 22 - Visibility of Lights

The lights prescribed in Rules (Subpart C) shall have an intensity as specified in Annex I to these Rules (33 CFR part 84), so as to be visible at the following minimum ranges:

(a) In vessels of 50 meters or more in length:

> (i) a masthead light, 6 miles;
> (ii) a sidelight, 3 miles;
> (iii) a sternlight, 3 miles;
> (iv) a towing light, 3 miles;
> (v) a white red, green or yellow all-round light, 3 miles; and
> ‹‹ *(vi) a special flashing light, 2 miles.* ››

(b) In vessels of 12 meters or more in length but less than 50 meters in length;

> (i) a masthead light, 5 miles; except that where the length of the vessel is less than 20 meters, 3 miles;
> (ii) a sidelight, 2 miles;
> (iii) a sternlight, 2 miles;
> (iv) a towing light, 2 miles;
> (v) a white, red, green or yellow all-round light, 2 miles; and
> ‹‹ *(vi) a special flashing light, 2 miles.* ››

(c) In vessels of less than 12 meters in length:

> (i) a masthead light, 2 miles;
> (ii) a sidelight, 1 mile;
> (iii) a sternlight, 2 miles;
> (iv) a towing light, 2 miles;
> (v) a white red, green or yellow all-round light, 2 miles; and
> ‹‹ *(vi) a special flashing light, 2 miles.* ››

(d) In inconspicuous, partly submerged vessels or objects being towed;

(i) a white all-round light; 3 miles.

Rule 23 - Power-driven Vessels Underway

(a) A power-driven vessel underway shall exhibit:

> (i) a masthead light forward;
> (ii) a second masthead light abaft of and higher than the forward one; except that a vessel of less than 50 meters in length shall not be obliged to exhibit such a light but may do so;

(iii) sidelights; and,

(iv) a sternlight.

(b) An air-cushion vessel when operating in non-displacement mode shall, in addition to the lights prescribed in Rule 23(a) 📷, exhibit an all-round flashing yellow light ‹‹ , where it can best be seen ››. 📷

(c) A WIG craft only when taking off, landing and in flight near the surface shall, in addition to the lights prescribed in Rule 23(a), exhibit a high intensity all-round flashing red light.

(d)(i) A power-driven vessel of less than 12 meters in length may in lieu of the lights prescribed in Rule 23(a) exhibit an all-round white light and sidelights. 📷

International

(ii) a power-driven vessel of less than 7 meters in length whose maximum speed does not exceed 7 knots may in lieu of the lights prescribed in Rule 23(a) exhibit an all-round white light and shall, if practicable, also exhibit sidelights. 📷

(iii) the masthead light or all-round white light on a power-driven vessel of less than 12 metres in length may be displaced from the fore and aft centre line of the vessel if centreline fitting is not practicable, provided that the sidelights are combined in one lantern which shall be carried on the fore and aft centre line of the vessel or located as nearly as practicable in the same fore and aft line as the masthead light or the all-round white light.

Inland

(e) A power-driven vessel when operating on the Great Lakes may carry an all-round white light in lieu of the second masthead light and sternlight prescribed in Rule 23(a). The light shall be carried in the position of the second masthead light and be visible at the same minimum range. 📷

Rule 24 - Towing and Pushing 🔝

(a) A power-driven vessel when towing astern shall exhibit: 📷

(i) Instead of the light prescribed in Rule 23(a)(i) or 23(a)(ii), two masthead lights in a vertical line. When the length of the tow, measuring from the stern of the towing vessel to the after end of the tow, exceeds 200 meters, three such lights in a vertical line;

(ii) sidelights;

(iii) a sternlight;

(iv) a towing light in a vertical line above the sternlight; and

(v) when the length of the tow exceeds 200 meters, a diamond shape where it can best be seen. 📷

(b) When a pushing vessel and a vessel being pushed ahead are rigidly connected in a composite unit they shall be regarded as a power-driven vessel and exhibit the lights prescribed in Rule 23. 📷

Interpretative Rule (33CFR 90.2‡82.2)

Rule 24(b) states that when a pushing vessel and a vessel being pushed ahead are rigidly connected in a composite unit, they are regarded as a power-driven vessel and must exhibit the lights prescribed in Rule 23. A "composite unit" is interpreted to be ‹‹ the combination of ›› a pushing vessel ‹ that is › ‹‹ and a vessel being pushed ahead that are ›› rigidly connected by mechanical means ‹ to a › ‹‹ so they react to sea and swell as one ›› vessel. Mechanical means does not include: lines, wires, hawsers, or chains.

(c) A power-driven vessel when pushing ahead or towing alongside, except ‹ in the case of a composite unit › ‹‹ as required by Rules 24(b) and (i) ››, shall exhibit:

(i) instead of the light prescribed in Rule 23(a)(i) or 23(a)(ii), two masthead lights in a vertical line;

(ii) sidelights; ‹‹ and ››

(iii) ‹ a sternlight › ‹‹ two towing lights in a vertical line ››.

(d) A power-driven vessel to which Rule 24(a) or (c) applies shall also comply with Rule 23 ‹‹ (a)(i) and ›› (a)(ii). 📷

(e) A vessel or object being towed 📷, other than those ‹ mentioned › ‹‹ referred ›› in Rule 24(g), shall exhibit:

(i) sidelights;

(ii) a sternlight; ‹‹ *and* ››

(iii) when the length of the tow exceeds 200 meters, a diamond shape where it can best be seen.

(f) Provided that any number of vessels being towed alongside or pushed in a group shall be lighted as one vessel ‹‹ *except as provided in Rule 24(f)(iii)* ››.

(i) a vessel being pushed ahead, not being part of a composite unit, shall exhibit at the forward end, sidelights, and ‹‹ *a special flashing light* ››;

(ii) a vessel being towed alongside shall exhibit a sternlight and at the forward end, sidelights, and ‹‹ *a special flashing light* ››;

Inland

(iii) when vessels are towed alongside on both sides of the towing vessel a sternlight shall be exhibited on the stern of the outboard vessel on each side of the towing vessel, and a single set of sidelights as far forward and as far outboard as is practicable, and a single special flashing light;

(g) An inconspicuous, partly submerged vessel or object, or combination of such vessels or objects being towed, shall exhibit:

(i) if it is less than 25 meters in breadth, one all-round white light at or near the forward end and one at or near the after end except that dracones need not exhibit a light at or near ‹ the forward › ‹‹ *each* ›› end.

International	Inland
(ii) if it is 25 meters or more in breadth, two or more additional all-round white lights at or near the extremities of its breadth;	*(ii) if it is 25 meters or more in breadth, four all-round white lights to mark its length and breadth;*

(iii) if it exceeds 100 meters in length, additional all-round white lights between the lights prescribed in Rule 24(g)(i) ‹‹ *and (ii)* ›› and so that the distance between the lights shall not exceed 100 meters ‹ ; › ‹‹ *: provided that any vessels or objects being towed alongside each other shall be lighted as one vessel or object;* ››

(iv) a diamond shape at or near the aftermost extremity of the last vessel or object being towed; and ‹ if the length of the tow exceeds 200 meters an additional diamond shape where it can best be seen and located as far forward as is practicable; ›

Inland

(v) the towing vessel may direct a searchlight in the direction of the tow to indicate its presence to an approaching vessel.

(h) Where from any sufficient cause it is impracticable for a vessel or object being towed to exhibit the lights or shapes prescribed in Rule 24(e) or (g), all possible measures shall be taken to light the vessel or object towed or at least to indicate the presence of ‹ such › ‹‹ *the unlighted* ›› vessel or object.

Interpretative Rule (33 CFR 90.7‡82.7)

An unmanned barge being towed may use the exception of COLREG Rule 24(h). However, this exception only applies to the vertical sector requirements.

(i) Where from any sufficient cause it is impracticable for a vessel not normally engaged in towing operations to display the lights prescribed in Rule 24(a), (c) ‹‹ *or (i)* ››, such vessel shall not be required to exhibit those lights when engaged in towing another vessel in distress or otherwise in need of assistance. All possible measures shall be taken to indicate the nature of the relationship between the towing vessel and the vessel being towed ‹ as authorized by Rule 36, in particular by illuminating the towline › ‹‹ *and the vessel being assisted. The searchlight authorized by Rule 36 may be used to illuminate the tow* ››.

Inland

(j) Notwithstanding Rule 24(c), on the Western Rivers (except below the Huey P. Long Bridge on the Mississippi River) and on waters specified by the Secretary*, a power-driven vessel when pushing ahead or towing alongside, except as Rule 24(b) applies, shall exhibit:

(i) sidelights; and

(ii) two towing lights in a vertical line.

Rule 25 - Sailing Vessels Underway and Vessels Under Oars

(a) A sailing vessel underway shall exhibit:

  (i) sidelights;
  (ii) a sternlight.

(b) In a sailing vessel of less than 20 meters in length the lights prescribed in Rule 25(a) may be combined in one lantern carried at or near the top of the mast where it can best be seen.

(c) A sailing vessel underway may, in addition to the lights prescribed in Rule 25(a), exhibit at or near the top of the mast, where they can best be seen, two all-round lights in a vertical line, the upper being red and the lower green, but these lights shall not be exhibited in conjunction with the combined lantern permitted by Rule 25(b).

(d)(i) A sailing vessel of less than 7 meter in length shall, if practicable, exhibit the lights prescribed in Rule 25(a) or (b), but if she does not, she shall ‹‹ *exhibit an all around white light or* ›› have ready at hand an electric torch or lighted lantern showing a white light which shall be exhibited in sufficient time to prevent collision.

  (ii) A vessel under oars may exhibit the lights prescribed in this rule for sailing vessels, but if she does not, she shall ‹‹ *exhibit an all around white light or* ›› have ready at hand an electric torch or lighted lantern showing a white light which shall be exhibited in sufficient time to prevent collision.

(e) A vessel proceeding under sail when also being propelled by machinery shall exhibit forward where it can best be seen a conical shape, apex downwards. ‹‹ *A vessel of less than 12 meters in length is not required to exhibit this shape, but may do so.* ››

Rule 26 - Fishing Vessels

(a) A vessel engaged in fishing, whether underway or at anchor, shall exhibit only the lights and shapes prescribed in this Rule.

(b) A vessel when engaged in trawling, by which is meant the dragging through the water of a dredge net or other apparatus used as a fishing appliance, shall exhibit:

  (i) two all-round lights in a vertical line, the upper being green and the lower white, or a shape consisting of two cones with their apexes together in a vertical line one above the other;
  (ii) a masthead light abaft of and higher than the all-round green light; a vessel of less than 50 meters in length shall not be obliged to exhibit such a light but may do so;
  (iii) when making way through the water, in addition to the lights prescribed in this paragraph, sidelights and a sternlight.

(c) A vessel engaged in fishing, other than trawling, shall exhibit:

  (i) two all-round lights in a vertical line, the upper being red and the lower white, or a shape consisting of two cones with their apexes together in a vertical line one above the other;
  (ii) when there is outlying gear extending more than 150 meters horizontally from the vessel, an all-round white light or a cone apex upwards in the direction of the gear.
  (iii) when making way through the water, in addition to the lights prescribed in this paragraph, sidelights and a sternlight.

International

(e) A vessel ‹ when › not engaged in fishing shall not exhibit the lights or shapes prescribed in this Rule, but only those prescribed for a vessel of her length.

‹‹ (f) Additional signals for fishing vessels in close proximity ›› {same as International Rules Annex II}

1‡(i) The lights mentioned herein shall ‹, if exhibited in pursuance of Rule 26(d), › be placed where they can best be seen. They shall be at least 0.9 meters apart but at a lower level than lights prescribed in Rule 26 ‹ (b)(i) and (c)(i) ›. The lights shall be visible all round the horizon at a distance of at least 1 mile but at a lesser distance from the lights prescribed by ‹ these Rules › *‹‹ Rule 26(a)-(c) ››* for fishing vessels.

2‡(ii) Signals for trawlers.

(a)‡(1) Vessels ‹ of 20 m or more in length › when engaged in trawling, whether using demersal or pelagic gear, ‹ shall › *‹‹ may ››* exhibit:

(i)‡(A) when shooting their nets: two white lights in a vertical line;
(ii)‡(B) when hauling their nets: one white light over one red light in a vertical line;
(iii)‡(C) when the net has come fast upon an obstruction: two red lights in a vertical line.

(b)‡(2) ‹ A › *‹‹ Each ››* vessel ‹ of 20 m or more in length › engaged in pair trawling ‹ shall › *‹‹ may ››* exhibit:

(i)‡(A) by night, a searchlight directed forward and in the direction of the other vessel of the pair;
(ii)‡(B) when shooting or hauling their nets or when their nets have come fast upon an obstruction, the lights prescribed in Rule 26 (f)(2)(a)‡(f)(ii)(1).

3‡(iii) Signals for purse seiners.

(a)‡(1) Vessels engaged in fishing with purse seine gear may exhibit two yellow lights in a vertical line. These lights shall flash alternately every second and with equal light and occultation duration. These lights may be exhibited only when the vessel is hampered by its fishing gear.

Rule 27 - Vessels Not Under Command or Restricted in Their Ability to Maneuver 🔔

(a) A vessel not under command shall exhibit:

(i) two all-round red lights in a vertical line where they can best be seen;
(ii) two balls or similar shapes in a vertical line where they can best be seen;
(iii) when making way through the water, in addition to the lights prescribed in this paragraph, sidelights and a sternlight.

(b) A vessel restricted in her ability to maneuver, except a vessel engaged in mineclearance operations, shall exhibit:

(i) three all-round lights in a vertical line where they can best be seen. The highest and lowest of these lights shall be red and the middle light shall be white;
(ii) three shapes in a vertical line where they can best be seen. The highest and lowest of these shapes shall be balls and the middle one a diamond.
(iii) when making way through the water, a masthead light(s), sidelights and a sternlight in addition to the lights prescribed in Rule 27(b)(i);
(iv) when at anchor, in addition to the lights or shapes prescribed in Rule 27(b)(i) and (ii), the light, lights, or shapes prescribed in Rule 30.

(c) A power-driven vessel engaged in a towing operation such as severely restricts the towing vessel and her tow in their ability to deviate from their course shall, in addition to the lights or shape prescribed in Rule 27(b)(i) and (ii), exhibit the lights or shape prescribed in Rule 24.

(d) A vessel engaged in dredging or underwater operations, when restricted in her ability to maneuver, shall exhibit the lights and shapes prescribed in Rules 27(b)(i), (ii) and (iii) and shall in addition when an obstruction exists, exhibit:

(i) two all-round red lights or two balls in a vertical line to indicate the side on which the obstruction exists;
(ii) two all-round green lights or two diamonds in a vertical line to indicate the side on which another vessel may pass; and
(iii) when at anchor, the lights or shapes prescribed in this paragraph instead of the lights or shapes prescribed in Rule 30.

Inland

(iv) Dredge pipelines that are floating or supported on trestles shall display the following lights at night and in periods of

restricted visibility.

(1) One row of yellow lights. The lights must be:

    (A) Flashing 50 to 70 times per minute,
    (B) Visible all round the horizon,
    (C) Visible for at least 2 miles,
    (D) Not less than 1 and not more than 3.5 meters above the water,
    (E) Approximately equally spaced, and
    (F) Not more than 10 meters apart where the pipeline crosses a navigable channel. Where the pipeline does not cross a navigable channel the lights must be sufficient in number to clearly show the pipeline's length and course.

(2) Two red lights at each end of the pipeline, including the ends in a channel where the pipeline is separated to allow vessels to pass (whether open or closed). The lights must be:

    (A) Visible all round the horizon, and
    (B) Visible for at least 2 miles, and
    (C) One meter apart in a vertical line with the lower light at the same height above the water as the flashing yellow light.

(e) Whenever the size of a vessel engaged in diving operations makes it impracticable to exhibit all lights and shapes prescribed in Rule 27(d), the following shall be exhibited:

    (i) Three all-round lights in a vertical line where they can best be seen. The highest and lowest of these lights shall be red and the middle light shall be white;
    (ii) a rigid replica of the International Code flag "A" not less than 1 meter in height. Measures shall be taken to ensure its all-round visibility.

(f) A vessel engaged in mine clearance operations shall, in addition to the lights prescribed for a power-driven vessel in Rule 23 or to the lights or shape prescribed for a vessel at anchor in Rule 30 as appropriate, exhibit three all-round green lights or three balls. One of these lights or shapes shall be exhibited near the foremast head and one at each end of the fore yard. These lights or shapes indicate that it is dangerous for another vessel to approach within 1000 meters of the mineclearance vessel.

(g) Vessels of less than 12 meters in length, except ‹ those › ‹‹ when ›› engaged in diving operations, ‹ shall not be › ‹‹ is not ›› required to exhibit the lights ‹ and › ‹‹ or ›› shapes prescribed in this Rule.

(h) The signals prescribed in this Rule are not signals of vessels in distress and requiring assistance. Such signals are contained in Annex IV to these Rules.

Rule 28 - Vessels Constrained by Their Draft

International
A vessel constrained by her draft may, in addition to the lights prescribed for power-driven vessels in Rule 23, exhibit where they can best be seen three all-round red lights in a vertical line, or a cylinder.

Rule 29 - Pilot Vessels

(a) A vessel engaged on pilotage duty shall exhibit:

    (i) at or near the masthead, two all-round lights in a vertical line, the upper being white and the lower red;
    (ii) when underway, in addition, sidelights and a sternlight;
    (iii) when at anchor, in addition to the lights prescribed in Rule 29(a)(i), the light, lights, or shape prescribed in Rule 30 for vessels at anchor.

(b) A pilot vessel when not engaged on pilotage duty shall exhibit the lights or shapes prescribed for a similar vessel of her length.

Rule 30 - Anchored Vessels and Vessels Aground

(a) A vessel at anchor shall exhibit where it can best be seen:

    (i) in the fore part, an all-round white light or one ball;
    (ii) at or near the stern and at a lower level than the light prescribed in Rule 30(a)(i), an all-round white light.

Interpretative Rule (33 CFR 90.5‡82.5)

‹ For the purposes of Rule 30 of the 72 COLREGS, › a "vessel at anchor" includes a ‹ barge › « vessel > made fast to one or more mooring buoys or other similar device attached to the ‹ sea or river › « ocean ›› floor. Such ‹ barge › « vessels ›› may be lighted as a vessel at anchor in accordance with Rule 30, or may be lighted on the corners in accordance with Rule 30(h)-(l).

(b) A vessel of less than 50 meters in length may exhibit an all-round white light where it can best be seen instead of the lights prescribed in Rule 30(a). 📷

(c) A vessel at anchor may, and a vessel of 100 meters and more in length shall, also use the available working or equivalent lights to illuminate her decks. 📷

(d) A vessel aground shall exhibit the lights prescribed in Rule 30(a) or (b) and in addition, if practicable, where they can best be seen; 📷

> (i) two all-round red lights in a vertical line;
> (ii) three balls in a vertical line.

(e) A vessel of less than 7 meters in length, when at anchor not in or near a narrow channel, fairway or where other vessels normally navigate, shall not be required to exhibit the lights or shape prescribed in Rule 30(a) and (b).

(f) A vessel of less than 12 meters in length, when aground, shall not be required to exhibit the lights or shapes prescribed in Rule 30(d) (i) and (ii).

Inland

(g) A vessel of less than 20 meters in length, when at anchor in a special anchorage area designated by the Coast Guard, shall not be required to exhibit the anchor lights and shapes required by this Rule.

(h) The following barges shall display at night and if practicable in periods of restricted visibility the lights described in Rule 30(i):

> *(i) Every barge projecting into a buoyed or restricted channel.*
> *(ii) Every barge so moored that it reduces the available navigable width of any channel to less than 80 meters.*
> *(iii) Barges moored in groups more than two barges wide or to a maximum width of over 25 meters.*
> *(iv) Every barge not moored parallel to the bank or dock.*

(i) Barges described in Rule 30(h) shall carry two unobstructed all-round white lights of an intensity to be visible for at least 1 nautical mile and meeting the technical requirements as prescribed in Annex I.

(j) A barge or a group of barges at anchor or made fast to one or more mooring buoys or other similar device, in lieu of the provisions of Rule 30, may carry unobstructed all-round white lights of an intensity to be visible for at least 1 nautical mile that meet the requirements of Annex I and shall be arranged as follows:

> *(i) Any barge that projects from a group formation, shall be lighted on its outboard corners.*
> *(ii) On a single barge moored in water where other vessels normally navigate on both sides of the barge, lights shall be placed to mark the corner extremities of the barge.*
> *(iii) On barges moored in group formation, moored in water where other vessels normally navigate on both sides of the group, lights shall be placed to mark the corner extremities of the group.*

(k) The following are exempt from the requirements of Rule 30:

> *(i) A barge or group of barges moored in a slip or slough used primarily for mooring purposes.*
> *(ii) A barge or group of barges moored behind a pierhead.*
> *(iii) A barge less than 20 meters in length when moored in a special anchorage area designated in accordance with 33 CFR 109.10.*

(l) Barges moored in well-illuminated areas are exempt from the lighting requirements of Rule 30. These areas are as follows:

CHICAGO SANITARY SHIP CANAL: (1) Mile 293.2 to 293.9; (2) Mile 295.2 to 296.1; (3) Mile 297.5 to 297.8; (4) Mile 298 to 298.2; (5) Mile 298.6 to 298.8; (6) Mile 299.3 to 299.4; (7) Mile 299.8 to 300.5; (8) Mile 303 to 303.2; (9) Mile 303.7 to 303.9; (10) Mile 305.7 to 305.8; (11) Mile 310.7 to 310.9; (12) Mile 311 to 311.2; (13) Mile 312.5 to 312.6; (14) Mile 313.8 to 314.2; (15) Mile 314.6; (16) Mile 314.8 to 315.3; (17) Mile 315.7 to 316; (18) Mile 316.8; (19) Mile 316.85 to 317.05; (20) Mile 317.5; (21) Mile 318.4 to 318.9; (22) Mile 318.7 to 318.8; (23) Mile 320 to 320.3; (24) Mile 320.6; (25) Mile 322.3 to 322.4; (26) Mile 322.8; (27) Mile 322.9 to 327.2

CALUMET SAG CHANNEL: (28) Mile 316.5

LITTLE CALUMET RIVER: (29) Mile 321.2; (30) Mile 322.3

CALUMET RIVER: (31) Mile 328.5 to 328.7; (32) Mile 329.2 to 329.4; (33) Mile 330 west bank to 330.2; (34) Mile 331.4 to 331.6; (35) Mile 332.2 to 332.4; (36) Mile 332.6 to 332.8

CUMBERLAND RIVER: (37) Mile 126.8; (38) Mile 191

Rule 31 - Seaplanes ⬆

Where it is impracticable for a seaplane or a WIG craft to exhibit lights or shapes of the characteristics or in the positions prescribed in Rules 20-31 she shall exhibit lights and shapes as closely similar in characteristics and position as is possible.

PART D - SOUND AND LIGHT SIGNALS

Rule 32 - Definitions ⬆

(a) The word "whistle" means any sound signaling appliance capable of producing the prescribed blasts and which complies with the specifications in Annex III to these Rules.

(b) The term "short blast" means a blast of about one seconds duration.

(c) The term "prolonged blast" means a blast of from four to six seconds duration.

Rule 33 - Equipment for Sound Signals (See also Annex III) ⬆

(a) A vessel of 12 meters or more in length shall be provided with a whistle, a vessel of 20 meters or more in length shall be provided with a bell in addition to a whistle, and a vessel of 100 meters or more in length shall, in addition be provided with a gong, the tone and sound of which cannot be confused with that of the bell. The whistle, bell and gong shall comply with the specifications in Annex III to these Regulations. The bell or gong or both may be replaced by other equipment having the same respective sound characteristics, provided that manual sounding of the prescribed signals shall always be possible.

(b) A vessel of less than 12 meters in length shall not be obliged to carry the sound signaling appliances prescribed in Rule 33(a) but if she does not, she shall be provided with some other means of making an efficient signal.

Rule 34 - Maneuvering and Warning Signals ⬆

International	Inland
(a) When vessels are in sight of one, a power-driven vessel underway, when maneuvering as authorized or required by these Rules, shall indicate that maneuver by the following signals on her whistle:	(a) When *power-driven* vessels are in sight of one another *and meeting or crossing at a distance within half a mile of each other, each* vessel underway, when maneuvering as authorized or required by these Rules, *(i)* shall indicate that maneuver by the following signals on her whistle:
–One short blasts to mean	
"I am altering my course to starboard"	*"I intend to leave you on my port side"*
–Two short blasts to mean	
"I am altering my course to port"	*"I intend to leave you on my starboard side"*
–Three short blasts to mean "I am operating astern propulsion"	
	(ii) upon hearing the one or two blast signal of the other shall, if in agreement, sound the same whistle signal and take the steps necessary to effect a safe passing. If,

	however, from any cause, the vessel doubts the safety of the proposed maneuver, she shall sound the signal specified in Rule 34(d) and each vessel shall take appropriate precautionary action until a safe passing agreement is made.

(b) ‹ Any › ‹‹ *A* ›› vessel may supplement the whistle signals prescribed in Rule 34(a) by light signals, ‹ repeated as appropriate, while the maneuver is being carried out: ›

(i) these signals shall have the following significance:
(ii) the duration of each flash shall be about one second ‹ , the interval between flashes shall be about one second, and the interval between successive signals shall not be less than ten seconds ›
(iii) the light used for this signal shall, if fitted, be an all-round white ‹‹ *or yellow* ››, visible at a minimum range of ‹ 5 › ‹‹ *2* ›› miles, ‹‹ *synchronized with the whistle* ›› and shall comply with the provisions of Annex I to these Regulations.

−One flash to mean	
"I am altering my course to starboard"	*"I intend to leave you on my port side"*

−Two flashes to mean	
"I am altering my course to port"	*"I intend to leave you on my starboard side"*

−Three flashes to mean
"I am operating astern propulsion"

(c) When in sight of one another in a narrow channel or fairway: (i) a vessel intending to overtake another shall in compliance with Rule 9(e)(i) indicate her intention by the following signals on her whistle:	(c) *When in sight of one another:* (i) *a* power-driven *vessel intending to overtake another power-driven vessel shall indicate her intention by the following signals on her whistle:*
−two prolonged blasts followed by one short blast to mean	−*one* short blast *to mean*

"I intend to overtake you on your starboard side"

−two prolonged blasts followed by two short blasts to mean	−*two* short blasts *to mean*

"I intend to overtake you on your port side"

(ii) the vessel about to be overtaken when acting in accordance with Rule 9(e)(i) shall indicate her agreement by the following signal on her whistle: −one prolonged, one short, one prolonged and one short blast, in that order.	(ii) *the power-driven vessel about to be overtaken shall, if in agreement, sound a similar sound signal. If in doubt she shall sound the signal prescribed in Rule 34(d).*

(d) When vessels in sight of one another are approaching each other and from any cause either vessel fails to understand the intentions or actions of the other, or is in doubt whether sufficient action is being taken by the other to avoid collision, the vessel in doubt shall immediately indicate such doubt by giving at least five short and rapid blasts on the whistle. Such signal may be supplemented by at least five short and rapid flashes.

(e) A vessel nearing a bend or an area of a channel or fairway where other vessels may be obscured by an intervening obstruction shall sound one prolonged blast. This signal shall be answered with a prolonged blast by any approaching vessel that may be within hearing around the bend or behind the intervening obstruction.

(f) If whistles are fitted on a vessel at a distance apart of more than 100 meters, one whistle only shall be used for giving maneuvering and warning signals.

	(g) When a power-driven vessel is leaving a dock or berth, she shall sound one prolonged blast.
	(h) A vessel that reaches agreement with another vessel in a head-on, crossing, or overtaking situation, as for example, by using the radiotelephone as prescribed by the Vessel Bridge-to-Bridge Radiotelephone Act (85 Stat. 164; 33 U.S.C. 1201 et seq.), is not obliged to sound the whistle signals prescribed by this Rule, but may do so. If agreement is not reached, then whistle signals shall be exchanged in a timely manner and shall prevail.

Rule 35 - Sound Signals in Restricted Visibility ⬆

In or near an area of restricted visibility, whether by day or night the signals prescribed in this Rule shall be used as follows:

(a) A power-driven vessel making way through the water shall sound at intervals of not more than 2 minutes one prolonged blast.

(b) A power-driven vessel underway but stopped and making no way through the water shall sound at intervals of no more than 2 minutes two prolonged blasts in succession with an interval of about 2 seconds between them.

(c) A vessel not under command, a vessel restricted in her ability to maneuver ‹‹ whether underway or at anchor ››, ‹ a vessel constrained by her draft › , a sailing vessel, a vessel engaged in fishing and a vessel engaged in towing or pushing another vessel shall, instead of the signals prescribed in Rule 35(a) or (b), sound at intervals of not more than 2 minutes three blasts in succession, namely one prolonged followed by two short blasts.

International
(d) A vessel engaged in fishing, when at anchor, and a vessel restricted in her ability to maneuver when carrying out her work at anchor, shall instead of the signals prescribed in Rule 35(g) sound the signal prescribed in Rule 35(c).

(e) A vessel towed or if more than one vessel is towed the last vessel of the tow, if manned, shall at intervals of not more than 2 minutes sound four blasts in succession, namely one prolonged followed by three short blasts. When practicable, this signal shall be made immediately after the signal made by the towing vessel.

(f) When a pushing vessel and a vessel being pushed ahead are rigidly connected in a composite unit they shall be regarded as a power-driven vessel and shall give the signals prescribed in Rule 35(a) or (b).

(g) A vessel at anchor shall at intervals of not more than 1 minute ring the bell rapidly for about 5 seconds. In a vessel 100 meters or more in length the bell shall be sounded in the forepart of the vessel and immediately after the ringing of the bell the gong shall be sounded rapidly for about 5 seconds in the after part of the vessel. A vessel at anchor may in addition sound three blasts in succession, namely one short, one long and one short blast, to give warning of her position and of the possibility of collision to an approaching vessel.

(h) A vessel aground shall give the bell signal and if required the gong signal prescribed in Rule 35(g) and shall, in addition, give three separate and distinct strokes on the bell immediately before and after the rapid ringing of the bell. A vessel aground may in addition sound an appropriate whistle signal.

(i) A vessel of 12 meters or more but less than 20 meters in length shall not be obliged to give the bell signals prescribed in Rule 35(g) and (h). However, if she does not, she shall make some other efficient sound signal at intervals of not more than 2 minutes.

(j) A vessel of less than 12 meters in length shall not be obliged to give the above mentioned signals but, if she does not, shall make some other efficient sound signal at intervals of not more than 2 minutes.

(k) A pilot vessel when engaged on pilotage duty may, in addition to the signals prescribed in Rule 35(a), (b) or (g), sound an identity signal consisting of four short blasts.

Inland
(l) The following vessels shall not be required to sound signals as prescribed in Rule 35(g) when anchored in a special anchorage area designated by the Coast Guard: *(i) a vessel of less than 20 meters in length; and*   *(ii) a barge, canal boat, scow, or other nondescript craft.*

Rule 36 - Signals to Attract Attention 🕯

If necessary to attract the attention of another vessel, any vessel may make light or sound signals that cannot be mistaken for any signal authorized elsewhere in these Rules, or may direct the beam of her searchlight in the direction of the danger, in such a way as not to embarrass any vessel. ‹ Any light to attract the attention of another vessel shall be such that it cannot be mistaken for any aid to navigation. For the purpose of this Rule the use of high intensity intermittent or revolving lights, such as strobe lights, shall be avoided.›

Rule 37 - Distress Signals 🖼 🕯

When a vessel is in distress and requires assistance she shall use or exhibit the signals described in Annex IV to these Rules.

ANNEX IV - Distress Signals (33 CFR 87) 🕯

1. ‹‹ *Need of assistance.* ››

The following signals, used or exhibited either together or separately, indicate distress and need of assistance:

(a) a gun or other explosive signal fired at intervals of about a minute;

(b) a continuous sounding with any fog-signaling apparatus;

(c) rockets or shells, throwing red stars fired one at a time at short intervals;

(d) a signal made by any signaling method consisting of the group . . . – – – . . . (SOS) in the Morse Code;

(e) a signal sent by radiotelephony consisting of the spoken word "Mayday";

(f) the International Code Signal of distress indicated by N.C.;

(g) a signal consisting of a square flag having above or below it a ball or anything resembling a ball;

(h) flames on the vessel (as from a burning tar barrel, oil barrel, etc.);

(i) a rocket parachute flare or a hand flare showing a red light;

(j) a smoke signal giving off orange-colored smoke;

(k) slowly and repeatedly raising and lowering arms outstretched to each side;

(l) a distress alert by means of digital selective calling (DSC) transmitted on:

   (i) VHF channel 70, or
   (ii) MF/HF on the frequencies 2187.5 kHz, 8414.5 kHz, 4207.5 kHz, 6312 kHz, 12577 kHz or 16804.5 kHz;

(m) a ship-to-shore distress alert transmitted by the ship's Inmarsat or other mobile satellite service provider ship earth station;

(n) signals transmitted by emergency position-indicating radio beacons;

(o) approved signals transmitted by radiocommunication systems, including survival craft radar transponders ‹‹ 'meeting the requirements of 47 CFR 80.1095 {search and rescue locating devices} ››.

‹‹ *(p) A high intensity white light flashing at regular intervals from 50 to 70 times per minute.* ››

2. ‹‹ Exclusive use. ›› 🕯

The use or exhibition of any of the foregoing signals except for the purpose of indicating distress and need of assistance and the use of other signals which may be confused with any of the above signals is prohibited.

3. ‹‹ Supplemental signals. ›› 🕯

Attention is drawn to the relevant sections of the International Code of Signals, the International Aeronautical and Maritime Search and Rescue Manual, Volume III, ‹ *the International Telecommunication Union Radio Regulations,* › and the following signals:

(a) A piece of orange-colored canvas with either a black square and circle or other appropriate symbol (for identification from the air);

(b) A dye marker.

PART E - EXEMPTIONS

Rule 38 - Exemptions ↰

International	Inland
Any vessel (or class of vessel) provided that she complies with the requirements of — the International Regulations for the Preventing of Collisions at Sea, 1960, the keel of which is laid or is at a corresponding stage of construction before the entry into force of these Regulations may be exempted from compliance therewith as follows:	*Any vessel or class of vessels, the keel of which was laid or which is at a corresponding stage of construction before December 24, 1980, provided that she complies with the requirements of —*
(a) The installation of lights with ranges prescribed in Rule 22, until 4 years after the date of entry into force of these Regulations.	*(a) The Act of June 7, 1897 (30 Stat. 96), as amended (33 U.S.C. 154-232) for vessels navigating the waters subject to that statute;*
(b) The installation of lights with color specifications as prescribed in §7 of Annex I to these Regulations, until 4 years after the entry into force of these Regulations.	*(b) §4233 of the Revised Statutes (33 U.S.C. 301-356) for vessels navigating the waters subject to that statute;*
(c) The repositioning of lights as a result of conversion from Imperial to metric units and rounding off measurement figures, permanent exemption.	*(c) The Act of February 8, 1895 (28 Stat. 645), as amended (33 U.S.C. 241-295) for vessels navigating the waters subject to that statute; or*

(d) (i) The repositioning of masthead lights on vessels of less than 150 meters in length, resulting from the prescriptions of §3 (a) of Annex I to these Regulations, permanent exemption.
    (ii) The repositioning of masthead lights on vessels of 150 meters or more in length, resulting from the prescriptions of §3 (a) of Annex I to these Regulations, until 9 years after the date of entry into force of these Regulations.
	(d) §§3, 4, and 5 of the Act of April 25, 1940 (54 Stat. 163), as amended (46 U.S.C. 526 b, c, and d) for motorboats navigating the waters subject to that statute; shall be exempted from compliance with the technical Annexes to these Rules as follows:
	    (i) The installation of lights with ranges prescribed in Rule 22, vessels of less than 20 meters in length are permanently exempt;
	    (ii) The installation of lights with color specifications as prescribed in §7 of Annex I to these Rules, until 4 years after the effective date of the Inland Navigational Rules Act of 1980 (Pub. L. 96-591), except that vessels of less than 20 meters in length are permanently exempt;
	    (iii) The repositioning of lights as a result of a conversion to metric units and rounding off of measurement figures, are permanently exempt.
	    (iv) The horizontal repositioning of masthead lights prescribed by Annex I to these Rules, vessels of less than 150 meters in length are permanently exempted.
	    (v) Power-driven vessels of 12 meters or more but less than 20 meters in length are permanently exempt from the provisions of Rule 23(a)(i) and 23(a)(iv) provided that, in place of these lights, the vessel exhibits a white light aft visible all-around the horizon.

International

(e) The repositioning of masthead lights resulting from the prescriptions of §2(b) of Annex I to these Regulations, until 9 years after the date of entry into force of these Regulations.

(f) The repositioning of sidelights resulting from the prescriptions of §2(g) and 3(b) of Annex I to these Regulations, until 9 years after the date of entry into force of these Regulations.

(g) The requirements for sound signal appliances prescribed in Annex II to these Regulations, until 9 years after the date of entry into force of these Regulations.

(h) The repositioning of all-round lights resulting from the prescription of §9(b) of Annex I to these Regulations, permanent exemption.

Implementing Rule (33 CFR 81.20)

Each vessel under the 72 COLREGS, except the vessels of the Navy, is exempt from the requirements of the 72 COLREGS to the limitation for the period of time stated in Rule 38 (a), (b), (c), (d), (e), (f), and (g) if: (a) Her keel is laid or is at a corresponding stage of construction before July 15, 1977; and (b) She meets the International Regulations for Preventing Collisions at Sea, 1960 (77 Stat. 194, 33 U.S.C. 1051-1094).

PART F - VERIFICATION OF COMPLIANCE WITH THE PROVISIONS OF THE CONVENTION {COLREGS only}

Rule 39 – Definitions 🕭

International

(a) "Audit" means a systematic, independent and documented process for obtaining audit evidence and evaluating it objectively to determine the extent to which audit criteria are fulfilled.

(b) "Audit Scheme" means the IMO {International Maritime Organization} Member State Audit Scheme established by the Organization and taking into account the guidelines developed by the Organization*.

(c) "Code for Implementation" means the IMO {International Maritime Organization} Instruments Implementation Code (III Code) adopted by the Organization by resolution A.1070(28).

(d) "Audit Standard" means the Code for Implementation.

Rule 40 - Application 🕭

International

Contracting Parties shall use the provisions of the Code for Implementation in the execution of their obligations and responsibilities contained in the present Convention.

Rule 41 - Verification of compliance 🕭

International

(a) Every Contracting Party shall be subject to periodic audits by the Organization in accordance with the audit standard to verify compliance with and implementation of the present Convention.

(b) The Secretary-General of the Organization shall have responsibility for administering the Audit Scheme, based on the guidelines developed by the Organization*.

(c) Every Contracting Party shall have responsibility for facilitating the conduct of the audit and implementation of a programme of actions to address the findings, based on the guidelines developed by the Organization*.

(d) Audit of all Contracting Parties shall be:
    (i) based on an overall schedule developed by the Secretary-General of the Organization, taking into account the guidelines developed by the Organization*; and
    (ii) conducted at periodic intervals, taking into account the guidelines developed by the Organization*.

---

* Refer to the Framework and Procedures for the IMO Member State Audit Scheme, adopted by the Organization by resolution A.1067(28).

ANNEX I - Positioning and Technical Details of Lights and Shapes (33 CFR 84) 🔔

1. Definitions. 🔔

(a) The term "height above the hull" means height above the uppermost continuous deck. This height shall be measured from the position vertically beneath the location of the light.

Inland

(b) High-speed craft means a craft capable of maximum speed in meters per second (m/s) equal to or exceeding: $3.7\nabla^{0.1667}$; where ∇ = displacement corresponding to the design waterline (cubic meters).

Note: The same formula expressed in pounds and knots is maximum speed in knots (kts) equal to exceeding 1.98(lbs) $3.7\nabla^{0.1667}$; where ∇=displacement corresponding to design waterline in pounds.

(c) The term "practical cut-off" means, for vessels 20 meters or more in length, 12.5 percent of the minimum luminous intensity (Table 14(b)) corresponding to the greatest range of visibility for which the requirements of Annex I are met.

(d) The term "Rule" or "Rules" has the same meaning as in Rule 3(r).

---

2. Vertical positioning and spacing of lights. 🔔

(a) On a power-driven vessel of 20 meters or more in length the masthead light shall be placed as follows:

 (i) The forward masthead light, or if only one masthead light is carried, then that light, at a height above the hull of not less than ‹ 6 › ‹‹ 5 ›› meters, and, if the breadth of the vessel exceeds ‹ 6 › ‹‹ 5 ›› meters, then at a height above the hull not less than such breadth, so however that the light need not be placed at a greater height above the hull than ‹ 12 › ‹‹ 8 ›› meters;
 (ii) when two masthead lights are carried the after one shall be at least ‹ 4.5 › ‹‹ 2 ›› meters vertically higher than the forward one.

(b) The vertical separation of the masthead lights of power-driven vessels shall be such that in all normal conditions of trim the after light will be seen over and separate from the forward light at a distance of 1000 meters from the stem when viewed from ‹ sea › ‹‹ *water* ›› level.

(c) The masthead light of a power-driven vessel of 12 meters but less than 20 meters in length shall be placed at a height above the gunwale of not less than 2.5 meters.

International	Inland
(d) A power-driven vessel of less than 12 meters in length may carry the uppermost light at a height of less than 2.5 meters above the gunwale. When, however, a masthead light is carried in addition to sidelights and a sternlight or the all-round light prescribed in Rule 23(d)(i) is carried in addition to sidelights, then such masthead light or all-round light shall be carried at least 1 meter higher than the sidelights.	*(d) The masthead light, or the all-round light described in Rule 23(d), of a power-driven vessel of less than 12 meters in length shall be carried at least 1 meter higher than the sidelights.*

(e) One of the two or three masthead lights prescribed for a power-driven vessel when engaged in towing or pushing another vessel shall be placed in the same position as either the forward masthead light or the after masthead light, provided that ‹ , if carried on the after mast, › the lowest after masthead light shall be at least ‹ 4.5 › ‹‹ 2 ›› meters vertically higher than the ‹‹ *highest* ›› forward masthead light.

(f)(i) The masthead lights or lights prescribed in Rule 23(a) shall be so placed as to be above and clear of all other lights and obstructions except as described in §(f)(ii).
 (ii) When it is impracticable to carry the all-round lights prescribed by Rule 27(b)(i) ‹ or Rule 28 › below the masthead lights, they may be carried above the after masthead light(s) or vertically in between the forward masthead light(s) and after masthead light(s), provided that in the latter case the requirement of §3(c) shall be complied with.

(g) The sidelights of a power-driven vessel shall be placed at ‹ a height above the hull not greater than three quarters of that of › ‹‹ *least one meter lower than* ›› the forward masthead light. They shall not be so low as to be interfered with by deck lights.

(h) The sidelights, if in a combined lantern and carried on a power-driven vessel of less than 20 meters in length, shall be placed not less than 1 meter below the masthead light.

(i) When the Rules prescribe two or three lights to be carried in a vertical line, they shall be spaced as follows:

(i) On a vessel of 20 meters in length or more such lights shall be spaced not less than ‹ 2 › ‹‹ *1* ›› meter apart, and the lowest of these lights shall, except where a towing light is required, be placed at a height of not less than 4 meters above the hull.
(ii) On a vessel of less than 20 meters in length such lights shall be spaced not less than 1 meter apart and the lowest of these lights shall, except where a towing light is required, be placed at a height of not less than 2 meters above the gunwale.
(iii) When three lights are carried they shall be equally spaced.

(j) The lower of the two all-round lights prescribed for a vessel when engaged in fishing shall be at a height above the sidelights not less than twice the distance between the two vertical lights.

(k) The forward anchor light prescribed in Rule 30(a)(i), when two are carried, shall not be less than 4.5 meters above the after one. On a vessel of 50 meters or more in length this forward anchor light shall be placed at a height or not less than 6 meters above the hull.

3. Horizontal positioning and spacing of lights. 🝔

(a) Except as specified in paragraph (e) of this section, when two masthead lights are prescribed for a power-driven vessel, the horizontal distance between them ‹ shall › ‹‹ *must* ›› not be less than one quarter of the length of the vessel but need not be more than 50 meters. The forward light ‹ shall › ‹‹ *must* ›› be placed not more than one half of the length of the vessel from the stem.

(b) On a power-driven vessel of 20 meters or more in length the sidelights shall not be placed in front of the forward masthead lights. They shall be placed at or near the side of the vessel.

(c) When the lights prescribed in Rule 27(b)(i) are placed vertically between the forward masthead light(s) and the after masthead light(s), these all-round lights shall be placed at a horizontal distance of not less than 2 meters from the fore and aft centerline of the vessel in the athwartship direction.

(d) When only one masthead light is prescribed for a power-driven vessel, this light ‹ shall › ‹‹ *must* ›› be exhibited forward of amidships. For a vessel of less than 20 meters in length, the vessel shall exhibit one masthead light as far forward as is practicable.

(e) On power-driven vessels 50 meters but less than 60 meters in length operated on the Western Rivers, and those {waters specified by the Secretary}, the horizontal distance between masthead lights shall not be less than 10 meters.

4. Details of location of direction-indicating lights for fishing vessels, dredgers and vessels engaged in underwater operations. 🝔

(a) The light indicating the direction of the outlying gear from a vessel engaged in fishing as prescribed in Rule 26(c)(ii) shall be placed at a horizontal distance of not less than 2 meters and not more than 6 meters away from the two all-round red and white lights. This light shall be placed not higher than the all-round white light prescribed in Rule 26(c)(i) and not lower than the sidelights.

(b) The lights and shapes on a vessel engaged in dredging or underwater operations to indicate the obstructed side and/or the side on which it is safe to pass, as prescribed in Rule 27(d)(i) and (ii), shall be placed at the maximum practical horizontal distance, but in no case less than 2 meters, from the lights or shapes prescribed in Rule 27(b)(i) and (ii). In no case shall the upper of these lights or shapes be at a greater height than the lower of the three lights or shapes prescribed in Rule 27(b)(i) and (ii).

5. Screens ‹ for sidelights › . 🝔

‡ (a) The sidelights of vessels of 20 meters or more in length shall be fitted with ‹ inboard screens painted › matt black, ‹‹ *inboard screens* ›› and meet‹ing› the requirements of §9‡15. On vessels of less than 20 meters in length, the sidelights, if necessary to meet the requirements of §9‡15, shall be fitted with ‹ inboard › matt black ‹‹ *inboard* ›› screens. With a combined lantern, using a single vertical filament and a very narrow division between the green and red sections, external screens need not be fitted.

(b) On power-driven vessels less than 12 meters in length constructed after July 31, 1983, the masthead light, or the all-round light described in Rule 23(d) shall be screened to prevent direct illumination of the vessel forward of the operator's position.

6. Shapes. ↰

(a) Shapes shall be black and of the following sizes:

(i) A ball shall have a diameter of not less than 0.6 meter;
(ii) a cone shall have a base diameter of not less than 0.6 meter‹s› and a height equal to its diameter;
‹ (iii) a cylinder shall have a diameter of at least 0.6 meter and a height of twice its diameter; ‹
(iv)‡(iii) a diamond shape shall consist of two cones as defined in §(a)(ii) having a common base.

(b) The vertical distance between shapes shall be at least 1.5 meter‹s›.

(c) In a vessel of less than 20 meters in length shapes of lesser dimensions but commensurate with the size of the vessel may be used and the distance apart may be correspondingly reduced.

‹ 7 › ‹‹ 13 ››. Color specification of lights. ↰

(a) The chromaticity of all navigation lights shall conform to the following standards, which lie within the boundaries of the area of the diagram specified for each color by the International Commission on Illumination (CIE).‹, in the "Colors of Light Signals", which is incorporated by reference. It is Publication CIE No. 2.2. (TC-1.6), 1975, and is available from the Illumination Engineering Society, 345 East 47th Street, New York, NY 10017 and is available for inspection at the Coast Guard, Shore Infrastructure Logistics Center, Aids to Navigation and Marine Environmental Response Product Line (CG-SILC-ATON/MER), 2703 Martin Luther King, Jr. Ave SE, Mailstop 7714, Washington, DC 20593-7714. It is also available for inspection at the National Archives and Records Administration (NARA). For information on the availability of this material at NARA, call 202-741-6030, or go to: http://www.archives.gov/federal_register/code_of_federal_regulations/ibr_locations.html. This incorporation by reference was approved by the Director of the Federal Register.›

(b) The boundaries of the area for each color are given by indicating the corner co-ordinates, which are as follows:

(i) White:

x	0.525	0.525	0.452	0.310	0.310	0.443
y	0.382	0.440	0.440	0.348	0.283	0.382

(ii) Green:

x	0.028	0.009	0.300	0.203
y	0.385	0.723	0.511	0.356

(iii) Red:

x	0.680	0.660	0.735	0.721
y	0.320	0.320	0.265	0.259

(iv) Yellow:

x	0.612	0.618	0.575	0.575
y	0.382	0.382	0.425	0.406

‹ 8 › ‹‹ 14 ››. Intensity of lights. ↰

(a) The minimum luminous intensity of lights shall be calculated by using the formula:

$$I = 3.43 \times 10^6 \times T \times D^2 \times K^{-D}$$

where:

I is luminous intensity in candelas under service conditions,
T is threshold factor 2×10^{-7} lux,
D is range of visibility (luminous range) of the light in nautical miles,
K is atmospheric transmissivity. For prescribed lights the value of K shall be 0.8, corresponding to a meteorological visibility of approximately 13 nautical miles.

(b) A selection of figures derived from the formula is given in the following table:

Range of visibility (luminous range) of light in nautical miles D	Minimum luminous intensity of light in candelas for K = 0.8 I
1	0.9
2	4.3
3	12
4	27
5	52

‹ Note: The maximum luminous intensity of navigation lights should be limited to avoid undue glare. This shall not be achieved by a variable control of the luminous intensity. ›

‹ 9 › ‹‹ 15 ››. Horizontal sectors. 🕭

(a)(i) In the forward direction, sidelights as fitted on the vessel shall show the minimum required intensities. The intensities shall decrease to reach practical cut-off between 1 and 3 degrees outside the prescribed sectors.

(ii) For sternlights and masthead lights and at 22.5 degrees abaft the beam for sidelights, the minimum required intensities shall be maintained over the arc of the horizon up to 5 degrees within the limits of the sectors prescribed in Rule 21. From 5 degrees within the prescribed sectors the intensity may decrease by 50 percent up to the prescribed limits; it shall decrease steadily to reach practical cut-off at not more than 5 degrees outside the prescribed sectors.

(b)(i) All-round lights shall be so located as not to be obscured by masts, topmasts or structures within angular sectors of more than 6 degrees, except anchor lights prescribed in Rule 30, which need not be placed at an impracticable height above the hull ‹‹ , and the all-round white light described in Rule 23(e), which may not be obscured at all ››.

(ii) If it is impracticable to comply with §(b)(i) by exhibiting only one all-round light, two all-round lights shall be used suitably positioned or screened so that they ‹‹ to ›› appear, as far as practicable, as one light at a ‹‹ minimum ›› distance of 1 ‹‹ nautical ›› mile.

‹‹ Note: Two unscreened all-round lights that are 1.28 meters apart or less will appear as one light to the naked eye at a distance of 1 nautical mile. ››

‹ 10 › ‹‹ 16 ››. Vertical sectors. 🕭

(a) The vertical sectors of electric lights as fitted, with the exception of lights on sailing vessels underway ‹‹ and on unmanned barges ››, shall ensure that:

(i) At least the required minimum intensity is maintained at all angles from 5 degrees above to 5 degrees below the horizontal;
(ii) at least 60 percent of the required minimum intensity is maintained from 7.5 degrees above to 7.5 degrees below the horizontal.

(b) In the case of sailing vessels underway the vertical sectors of electric lights as fitted shall ensure that:

(i) At least the required minimum intensity is maintained at all angles from 5 degrees above to 5 degrees below the horizontal;
(ii) at least 50 percent of the required minimum intensity is maintained from 25 degrees above to 25 degrees below the horizontal.

Inland
(c) In the case of unmanned barges the minimum required intensity of electric lights as fitted shall be maintained on the horizontal.

(c)‡(d) In the case of lights other than electric lights these specifications shall be met as closely as possible.

‹ 11 › ‹‹ 17 ››. Intensity of non-electric lights. 🕭

Non-electric lights shall so far as practicable comply with the minimum intensities, as specified in the ‹‹ Intensity of Lights ›› Table.

‹ 12 › ‹‹ 18 ››. Maneuvering light. 🕭

‹‹ Notwithstanding the provisions of §2(f) ››, the maneuvering light described in Rule 34(b) shall be placed ‹‹ approximately ›› in the same fore and aft vertical plane as the masthead light or lights and, where practicable, at a minimum height of ‹ 2 › ‹‹ 1.5 ›› meter vertically above the forward masthead light, provided that it shall be carried not less than ‹ 2 › ‹‹ 1.5 ›› meter vertically above or below the after masthead light. On a vessel where only one masthead light is carried, the maneuvering light, if fitted, shall be carried where it can best be seen, not less than ‹ 2 › ‹‹ 1.5 ›› meters vertically apart from the masthead light.

‹ 13 › ‹‹ 19 ››. High-speed Craft. 🕭

(a) The masthead light of high-speed craft may be placed at a height related to the breadth ‹‹ of the craft ›› lower than that prescribed in §2(a)(i), provided that the base angle of the isosceles triangle formed by the sidelights and masthead light when seen in end elevation is not less than 27 degrees.

(b) On high-speed craft of 50 meters or more in length, the vertical separation between foremast and mainmast light of 4.5 meters required by §2(a)(ii) {editorial correction; amending §2(k) in 33 CFR §84.19 to §2(a)(ii) pends rulemaking} may be modified provided that such distance shall not be less than the value determined by the following formula:

$$y = \frac{(a+17\Psi)C}{1000} + 2$$

where:
- y   is the height of the mainmast light above the foremast light in meters;
- a   is the height of the foremast light above the water surface in service condition in meters;
- Y   is the trim in service condition in degrees;
- C   is the horizontal separation of masthead lights in meters.

Note: Refer to the International Code of Safety for High-Speed Craft, 1994 and the International Code of Safety for High-Speed Craft, 2000.

‹ 14 › ‹‹ *20* ››. **Approval.** ↰

The construction of lights and shapes and the installation of lights on board the vessel ‹ shall be to the satisfaction of the appropriate authority of the State whose flag the vessel is entitled to fly › ‹‹ *must satisfy the Commandant, U. S. Coast Guard* ››.

ANNEX II - Additional Signals for Fishing Vessels Fishing In Close Proximity {at Rule 26(f)} ↰

ANNEX III - Technical Details of Sound Signal Appliances (33 CFR 86) ↰

1. Whistles. ↰

(a) Frequencies and range of audibility. The fundamental frequency of the signal shall lie within the range 70-700 Hz. The range of audibility of the signal from a whistle shall be determined by those frequencies, which may include the fundamental and/or one or more higher frequencies, which lie within the range 180-700 Hz (+/- 1 percent) for a vessel of 20 meters or more in length, or 180-2100 Hz (+/- 1 percent) for a vessel of less than 20 meters in length and which provide the sound pressure levels specified in §1(c).

(b) Limits of fundamental frequencies. To ensure a wide variety of whistle characteristics, the fundamental frequency of a whistle shall be between the following limits:

- (i) 70-200 Hz, for a vessel 200 meters or more in length;
- (ii) 130-350 Hz, for a vessel 75 meters but less than 200 meters in length;
- (iii) 250-700 Hz, for a vessel less than 75 meters in length.

(c) Sound signal intensity and range of audibility. A whistle fitted in a vessel shall provide, in the direction of maximum intensity of the whistle and at a distance of 1 meter from it, a sound pressure level in at least one one-third octave band within the range of frequencies 180-700 Hz (+/- 1 percent) for a vessel of 20 meters ‹ or more in length, or 180-2100 Hz (+/- 1 percent) for a vessel of less than 20 meters in length ›, of not less than the appropriate figure given in the table below.

Length of vessel in meters	One-third octave band level at 1 meter in dB referred to 2×10^{-5}N/m^2	Audibility range in nautical miles
200 or more	143	2
75 but less than 200	138	1.5
20 but less than 75	130	1
Less than 20	120* 115** 111***	0.5

* When the measured frequencies lie within the range 180-450 Hz

** When the measured frequencies lie within the range 450-800 Hz

*** When the measured frequencies lie within the range 800-2100 Hz

The range of audibility in the table is for information and is approximately the range at which a whistle may be heard on its forward axis with 90 percent probability in conditions of still air on board a vessel having average background noise level at the listening posts (taken to be 68 dB in the octave band centered on 250 Hz and 63 dB in the octave band centered on 500 Hz). ‹‹ *It is shown for informational purposes only.* ›› In practice, the range at which a whistle may be heard is extremely variable and depends critically on weather conditions; the values given can be regarded as typical but under conditions of strong wind or high ambient noise level at the listening post the range may be reduced.

(d) Directional properties. The sound pressure level of a directional whistle shall be not more than 4 dB below the ‹ prescribed › sound pressure level ‹ on the axis at ›, ‹‹ specified in §(c) ›› any direction in the horizontal plane within +/- 45 degrees of the axis. The sound pressure level ‹ at › ‹‹ of the whistle in ›› any other direction in the horizontal plane shall be not more than 10 dB ‹ below the prescribed sound pressure level on › ‹‹ *less than the sound pressure level specified for* ›› the forward axis, so that the range ‹‹ *audibility* ›› in any direction will be at least half the range ‹‹ *required* ›› on the forward axis. The sound pressure level shall be measured in that one-third octave band which determines the audibility range.

(e) Positioning of whistles.

(i) When a directional whistle is to be used as the only whistle on ‹ a vessel, it shall be installed with its maximum intensity directed straight ahead › ‹‹ *the vessel and is permanently installed, it shall be installed with its forward axis directed forward* ››.
(ii) A whistle shall be placed as high as practicable on a vessel, in order to reduce interception of the emitted sound by obstructions and also to minimize hearing damage risk to personnel. The sound pressure level of the vessel's own signal at listening posts shall not exceed 110 dB(A) and so far as practicable should not exceed 100 dB(A).

(f) Fitting of more than one whistle. If whistles are fitted at a distance apart of more than 100 meters, ‹ it shall be so arranged that they are › ‹‹ *they shall* ›› not ‹‹ *be* ›› sounded simultaneously.

International	Inland
(g) Combined whistle systems. If due to the presence of obstructions the sound field of a single whistle or of one of the whistles referred to in §(f) is likely to have a zone of greatly reduced signal level, it is recommended that a combined whistle system be fitted so as to overcome this reduction. The whistles of a combined system shall be located at a distance apart of not more than 100 meters and arranged to be sounded simultaneously. The frequency of any one whistle shall differ from those of the others by at least 10 Hz.	*(g) Combined whistle systems.* *(i) A combined whistle system is a number of whistles (sound emitting sources) operated together. For the purposes of the Rules of Subchapter E a combined whistle system is to be regarded as a single whistle.* *(ii) The whistles of a combined system shall:* *(1) Be located at a distance apart of not more than 100 meters;* *(2) Be sounded simultaneously;* *(3) Each have a fundamental frequency different from those of the others by at least 10 Hz; and* *(4) Have a tonal characteristic appropriate for the length of vessel which shall be evidenced by at least two-thirds of the whistles in the combined system having fundamental frequencies falling within the limits prescribed in paragraph (b) of this section, or if there are only two whistles in the combined system, by the higher fundamental frequency falling within the limits prescribed in paragraph (b) of this section.* *Note to paragraph (g): If, due to the presence of obstructions, the sound field of a single whistle or of one of the whistles referred to in paragraph (f) of this section is likely to have a zone of greatly reduced signal level, a combined whistle system should be fitted so as to overcome this reduction.*

Inland
(h) Towing vessel whistles. *A power-driven vessel normally engaged in pushing ahead or towing alongside may, at all times, use a whistle whose characteristic falls within the limits prescribed by §1(b) for the longest customary composite length of the vessel and its tow.*

2. Bell or gong. ↟

(a) Intensity of signal. A bell or gong, or other device having similar sound characteristics shall produce a sound pressure level of not less than 110 dB at ‹ a distance of › 1 meter ‹ from it ›.

(b) Construction. Bells and gongs shall be made of corrosion-resistant material and designed to give clear tone. The diameter of the mouth of the bell shall be not less than 300 mm for vessels of 20 meters or more in length. Where practicable, a power-driven bell striker is recommended to ensure constant force but manual operation shall be possible. The mass of the striker shall be not less than 3 percent of the mass of the bell.

International

3. Approval
The construction of sound signal appliances, their performance and their installation on board the vessel shall be to the satisfaction of the appropriate authority of the State whose flag the vessel is entitled to fly.

ANNEX IV - Distress Signals {at Rule 37} 🖒

ANNEX V – Pilot Rules {at Rule 22} 🖒

***

OTHER ASSOCIATED REFERENCES 🖒

ALTERNATIVE COMPLIANCE (33 CFR 81‡89) 🖒

1. Definitions. 🖒

As used in this part:

International	*Inland*
"72 COLREGS" refers to the International Regulations for Preventing Collisions at Sea, 1972, done at London, October 20, 1972, as rectified by the Proces-Verbal of December 1, 1973, as amended.	*"Inland Rules" refers to the Inland Navigation Rules contained in the Inland Navigational Rules Act of 1980 (Pub. L. 96-591) and the technical annexes established under that Act.*

A "vessel of special construction or purpose" means a vessel designed or modified to perform a special function and whose arrangement is thereby made relatively inflexible.

"Interference with the special function of the vessel" occurs when installation or use of lights, shapes, or sound-signaling appliances under the ‹ 72 COLREGS › ‹‹ *Inland Rules* ›› prevents or significantly hinders the operation in which the vessel is usually engaged.

3. General. 🖒

Vessels of special construction or purpose which cannot fully comply with the light, shape, and sound signal provisions of the Rules without interfering with their special function may instead meet alternative requirements. The Chief of the Prevention Division in each Coast Guard District Office makes this determination and requires that alternative compliance be as close as possible with the Rules. These regulations set out the procedure by which a vessel may be certified for alternative compliance. The information collection and recordkeeping requirements in §§5 and 18 have been approved by the Office of Management and Budget under OMB control No. 1625-0019.

5. Application For a Certificate of alternative compliance. 🖒

(a) The owner, builder, operator, or agent of a vessel of special construction or purpose who believes the vessel cannot fully comply with the Rules light, shape, or sound signal provisions without interference with its special function may apply for a determination that alternative compliance is justified. The application must be in writing, submitted to the Chief of the Prevention Division of the Coast Guard District in which the vessel is being built or operated, and include the following information:

    (1) The name, address, and telephone number of the applicant.

    (2) The identification of the vessel by its:

        (i) Official number;
        (ii) Shipyard hull number;
        (iii) Hull identification number; or
        (iv) State number, if the vessel does not have an official number or hull identification number.

(3) Vessel name and home port, if known.

(4) A description of the vessel's area of operation.

(5) A description of the provision for which the Certificate of Alternative Compliance is sought, including:

    (i) the Rules or Annex section number for which the Certificate of Alternative Compliance is sought;
    (ii) a description of the special function of the vessel that would be interfered with by full compliance with the provision of that Rule or Annex section; and
    (iii) a statement of how full compliance would interfere with the special function of the vessel.

(6) A description of the alternative installation that is in closest possible compliance with the applicable Rules Rule or Annex section.

(7) A copy of the vessel's plans or an accurate scale drawing that clearly shows:

    (i) the required installation of the equipment under the Rules ,
    (ii) the proposed installation of the equipment for which certification is being sought, and
    (iii) any obstructions that may interfere with the equipment when installed in:

        (A) the required location; and
        (B) the proposed location.

(b) The Coast Guard may request from the applicant additional information concerning the application.

9. Certificate of alternative compliance: contents. ⮭

The Chief of the Prevention Division issues the Certificate of Alternative Compliance to the vessel based on a determination that it cannot comply fully with Rules light, shape, and sound signal provisions without interference with its special function. This Certificate includes:

(a) Identification of the vessel as supplied in the application under §5(a)(2);

(b) The provision of the Rules for which the Certificate authorizes alternative compliance;

(c) A certification that the vessel is unable to comply fully with the Rules light, shape, and sound signal requirements without interference with its special function;

(d) A statement of why full compliance would interfere with the special function of the vessel;

(e) The required alternative installation;

(f) A statement that the required alternative installation is in the closest possible compliance with the Rules without interfering with the special function of the vessel;

(g) The date of issuance;

(h) A statement that the Certificate of Alternative Compliance terminates when the vessel ceases to be usually engaged in the operation for which the certificate is issued.

17. Certificate of alterative compliance: termination. ⮭

The Certificate of Alternative Compliance terminates if the information supplied under §5(a) or the Certificate issued under §9 is no longer applicable to the vessel.

18. Notice and record of certification of vessels of special construction or purpose. ⮭

International

(a) In accordance with 33 U.S.C. 1605(c), a notice is published in the Federal Register if the following:
 	
    (i) each Certificate of Alternative Compliance issued under §9; and
    (ii) each Coast Guard vessel determined by the Commandant to be a vessel of special construction or purpose.

  (b)‡(a) Copies of Certificates of Alternative Compliance and documentation concerning Coast Guard vessels are available for inspection at the offices of the Marine Transportation Systems Directorate, U.S. Coast Guard Headquarters (CG–5PW), Stop 7509, 2703 Martin Luther King Ave SE, Washington, DC 20593–7509.

(c)‡(b) The owner or operator of a vessel issued a certificate shall ensure that the vessel does not operate unless the Certificate of Alternative Compliance or a certified copy of that certificate is on board the vessel and available for inspection by Coast Guard personnel.

PENALTIES: Civil Penalties (33 U.S.C 1608) ‡ Violations of Inland Navigational Rules (33 U.S.C 2072) ℒ

(a) Liability of operator for civil penalty. Whoever operates a vessel in violation of this chapter ‹‹ *or of any regulation issued thereunder, or in violation of a certificate of alternative compliance issued under Rule 1* ›› is liable to a civil penalty of not more than $5,000 for each violation.

(b) Liability of vessel for ‹ violations › ‹‹ *civil penalties* ››; seizure of vessel. Every vessel subject to ‹ the provisions of › this chapter other than a public vessel being used for noncommercial purposes, ‹ which › ‹‹ *that* ›› is operated in violation of this chapter or of any regulation ‹ promulgated pursuant to §1607, shall be › ‹‹ *issued there under, or in violation of a certificate of alternative compliance issued under {Inland} Rule 1 is* ›› liable to a civil penalty of not more than $5,000 for each such violation, for which penalty the vessel may be seized and proceeded against in the district court of the United States of any district within which such vessel may be found.

(c) Assessment of ‹ penalties; notice; opportunity for hearing; remission, mitigation, and compromise of penalty; action for › ‹‹ civil penalty by Secretary; ›› collection. The Secretary ‹ of the department in which the Coast Guard is operating › may assess any civil penalty authorized by this section. No such penalty may be assessed until the person charged, or the owner of the vessel charged, as appropriate, shall have been given notice of the violation involved and an opportunity for a hearing. For good cause shown, the Secretary may remit, mitigate, or compromise any penalty assessed. Upon the failure of the person charged, or the owner of the vessel charged, to pay an assessed penalty, as it may have been mitigated or compromised, the Secretary may request the Attorney General to commence an action in the appropriate district court of the United States for collection of the penalty as assessed, without regard to the amount involved, together with such other relief as may be appropriate.

Inland

(d) Withholding of clearance.

(1) If any owner, operator, or individual in charge of a vessel is liable for a penalty under this section, or if reasonable cause exists to believe that the owner, operator, or individual in charge may be subject to a penalty under this section, the Secretary of the Treasury, upon the request of the Secretary, shall with respect to such vessel refuse or revoke any clearance required by §60105 of Title 46.

(2) Clearance or a permit refused or revoked under this subsection may be granted upon filing of a bond or other surety satisfactory to the Secretary.

PENALTIES FOR NEGLIGENT OPERATIONS AND INTERFERING WITH SAFE OPERATION (33 U.S.C 2302) ℒ

(a) A person operating a vessel in a negligent manner or interfering with the safe operation of a vessel, so as to endanger the life, limb, or property of a person is liable to the United States Government for a civil penalty of not more than $5,000 in the case of a recreational vessel, or $25,000 in the case of any other vessel.

(b) A person operating a vessel in a grossly negligent manner that endangers the life, limb, or property of a person commits a class A misdemeanor.

(c) An individual who is under the influence of alcohol, or a dangerous drug in violation of a law of the United States when operating a vessel, as determined under standards prescribed by the Secretary by regulation—

(1) is liable to the United States Government for a civil penalty of not more than $5,000; or
(2) commits a class A misdemeanor.

(d) For a penalty imposed under this section, the vessel also is liable in rem unless the vessel is—

(1) owned by a State or a political subdivision of a State;
(2) operated principally for governmental purposes; and
(3) identified clearly as a vessel of that State or subdivision.

(e)

(1) A vessel may not transport Government-impelled cargoes if—

(A) the vessel has been detained and determined to be substandard by the Secretary for violation of an international safety convention to which the United States is a party, and the Secretary has published notice of that detention and determination in an electronic form, including the name of the owner of the vessel; or

(B) the operator of the vessel has on more than one occasion had a vessel detained and determined to be substandard by the Secretary for violation of an international safety convention to which the United States is a party, and the Secretary has published notice of that detention and determination in an electronic form, including the name of the owner of the vessel.

(2) The prohibition in §(1) expires for a vessel on the earlier of—

(A) one year after the date of the publication in electronic form on which the prohibition is based; or

(B) any date on which the owner or operator of the vessel prevails in an appeal of the violation of the relevant international convention on which the detention is based.

VESSEL BRIDGE-TO-BRIDGE RADIOTELEPHONE REGULATIONS (33 CFR 26) ⮝

---

1. Purpose. ⮝

(a) The purpose of this part is to implement the provisions of the Vessel Bridge-to-Bridge Radiotelephone Act. This part:

(1) Requires the use of the vessel bridge-to-bridge radiotelephone;
(2) Provides the Coast Guard's interpretation of the meaning of important terms in the Act;
(3) Prescribes the procedures for applying for an exemption from the Act and the regulations issued under the Act and a listing of exemptions.

(b) Nothing in this part relieves any person from the obligation of complying with the rules of the road and the applicable pilot rules.

2. Definitions. ⮝

For the purpose of this part and interpreting the Act:

"Act" means the "Vessel Bridge-to-Bridge Radiotelephone Act", 33 U.S.C. §§1201-1208;
"Length" is measured from end to end over the deck excluding sheer;
"Power-driven vessel" means any vessel propelled by machinery; and
"Secretary" means the Secretary of the Department in which the Coast Guard is operating;
"Territorial sea" means all waters as defined in {33 CFR} §2.22(a)(1).
"Towing vessel" means any commercial vessel engaged in towing another vessel astern, alongside, or by pushing ahead.
"Vessel Traffic Services (VTS)" means a service implemented under 33 CFR 161 by the United States Coast Guard designed to improve the safety and efficiency of vessel traffic and to protect the environment. The VTS has the capability to interact with marine traffic and respond to traffic situations developing in the VTS area.
"Vessel Traffic Service Area or VTS Area" means the geographical area encompassing a specific VTS area of service as described in 33 CFR 161. This area of service may be subdivided into sectors for the purpose of allocating responsibility to individual Vessel Traffic Centers or to identify different operating requirements.

Note: Although regulatory jurisdiction is limited to the navigable waters of the United States, certain vessels will be encouraged or may be required, as a condition of port entry, to report beyond this area to facilitate traffic management within the VTS area.

3. Radiotelephone required. ⮝

(a) Unless an exemption is granted under §9 and except as provided in §(a)(4) of this section, this part applies to:

(1) Every power-driven vessel of 20 meters or over in length while navigating;
(2) Every vessel of 100 gross tons and upward carrying one or more passengers for hire while navigating;
(3) Every towing vessel of 26 feet or over in length while navigating; and
(4) Every dredge and floating plant engaged in or near a channel or fairway in operations likely to restrict or affect navigation of other vessels except for an unmanned or intermittently manned floating plant under the control of a dredge.

(b) Every vessel, dredge, or floating plant described in §(a) of this section must have a radiotelephone on board capable of operation from its navigational bridge, or in the case of a dredge, from its main control station, and capable of transmitting and receiving on the frequency or frequencies within the 156-162 Mega-Hertz band using the classes of emissions designated by the Federal Communications Commission for the exchange of navigational information.

(c) The radiotelephone required by §(b) of this section must be carried on board the described vessels, dredges, and floating plants upon the navigable waters of the United States.

(d) The radiotelephone required by §(b) of this section must be capable of transmitting and receiving on VHF FM channel 22A (157.1 MHz).

(e) While transiting any of the following waters, each vessel described in §(a) of this section also must have on board a radiotelephone capable of transmitting and receiving on VHF FM channel 67 (156.375 MHz):

(1) The lower Mississippi River from the territorial sea boundary, and within either the Southwest Pass safety fairway or the South Pass safety fairway specified in 33 CFR 166.200, to mile 242.4 AHP (Above Head of Passes) near Baton Rouge;

(2) The Mississippi River-Gulf Outlet from the territorial sea boundary, and within the Mississippi River-Gulf outlet Safety Fairway specified in 33 CFR 166.200, to that channel's junction with the Inner Harbor Navigation Canal; and

(3) The full length of the Inner Harbor Navigation Canal from its junction with the Mississippi River to that canal's entry to Lake Pontchartrain at the New Seabrook vehicular bridge.

(f) In addition to the radiotelephone required by §(b) of this section, each vessel described in §(a) of this section while transiting any waters within a Vessel Traffic Service Area, must have on board a radiotelephone capable of transmitting and receiving on the VTS designated frequency in Table 161.12(c) (VTS and VMRS Centers, Call Signs/MMSI, Designated Frequencies, and Monitoring Areas).

Note: A single VHF-FM radio capable of scanning or sequential monitoring (often referred to as "dual watch" capability) will not meet the requirements for two radios.

4. Use of the designated frequency. ↰

(a) No person may use the frequency designated by the Federal Communications Commission under §8 of the Act, 33 U.S.C. 1207(a), to transmit any information other than information necessary for the safe navigation of vessels or necessary tests.

(b) Each person who is required to maintain a listening watch under §5 of the Act shall, when necessary, transmit and confirm, on the designated frequency, the intentions of his vessel and any other information necessary for the safe navigation of vessels.

(c) Nothing in these regulations may be construed as prohibiting the use of the designated frequency to communicate with shore stations to obtain or furnish information necessary for the safe navigation of vessels.

(d) On the navigable waters of the United States, channel 13 (156.65 MHz) is the designated frequency required to be monitored in accordance with §5(a) except that in the area prescribed in §3(e), channel 67 (156.375 MHz) is the designated frequency.

(e) On those navigable waters of the United States within a VTS area, the designated VTS frequency is an additional designated frequency required to be monitored in accordance with §5.

5. Use of radiotelephone. ↰

§5 of the Act states that the radiotelephone required by this Act is for the exclusive use of the master or person in charge of the vessel, or the person designated by the master or person in charge to pilot or direct the movement of the vessel, who shall maintain a listening watch on the designated frequency. Nothing herein shall be interpreted as precluding the use of portable radiotelephone equipment to satisfy the requirements of this act.

6. Maintenance of radiotelephone; failure of radiotelephone. ↰

§6 of the Act states:

(a) Whenever radiotelephone capability is required by this Act, a vessel's radiotelephone equipment shall be maintained in effective operating condition. If the radiotelephone equipment carried aboard a vessel ceases to operate, the master shall exercise due diligence to restore it or cause it to be restored to effective operating condition at the earliest practicable time. The failure of a vessel's radiotelephone equipment shall not, in itself, constitute a violation of this Act, nor shall it obligate the master of any vessel to moor or anchor his vessel; however, the loss of radiotelephone capability shall be given consideration in the navigation of the vessel.

7. Communications. ↰

No person may use the services of, and no person may serve as, a person required to maintain a listening watch under §5 of the Act, 33 U.S.C. 1204, unless the person can communicate in the English language.

8. Exemption procedures. ↰

(a) The Commandant has redelegated to the Assistant Commandant for Prevention Policy, U.S. Coast Guard Headquarters, with the reservation that this authority shall not be further redelegated, the authority to grant exemptions from provisions of the Vessel Bridge-to-Bridge Radiotelephone Act and this part.

(b) Any person may petition for an exemption from any provision of the Act or this part;

(c) Each petition must be submitted in writing to Commandant (CG-DCO-D), Attn: Deputy for Operations Policy and Capabilities, U.S. Coast Guard Stop 7318, 2703 Martin Luther King Jr. Avenue SE., Washington, DC 20593-7318, and must state:

(1) The provisions of the Act or this part from which an exemption is requested; and

(2) The reasons why marine navigation will not be adversely affected if the exemption is granted and if the exemption relates to a local communication system how that system would fully comply with the intent of the concept of the Act but would not conform in detail if the exemption is granted.

9. List of exemptions. ⤴

(a) All vessels navigating on those waters governed by the navigation rules for Great Lakes and their connecting and tributary waters (33 U.S.C. 241 et seq.) are exempt from the requirements of the Vessel Bridge-to-Bridge Radiotelephone Act and this part until May 6, 1975.

(b) Each vessel navigating on the Great Lakes as defined in the Inland Navigational Rules Act of 1980 (33 U.S.C. 2001 et seq.) and to which the Vessel Bridge-to-Bridge Radiotelephone Act (33 U.S.C. 1201-1208) applies is exempt from the requirements in 33 U.S.C. 1203, 1204, and 1205 and the regulations under §§3, 4, 5, 6, and 7. Each of these vessels and each person to whom 33 U.S.C. 1208(a) applies must comply with Articles VII, X, XI, XII, XIII, XV, and XVI and Technical Regulations 1-9 of "The Agreement Between the United States of America and Canada for Promotion of Safety on the Great Lakes by Means of Radio, 1973."

LEGAL REFERENCES AND AMENDMENTS TO THE RULES ⤴

International	Inland
<ul><li>International Navigational Rules Act of 1977, see 91 stat. 308, 33 U.S.C. 1601 - 1608</li><li>Amendments to the International Navigation Rules (72 COLREGS), International Maritime Organization (IMO) resolutions:<ul><li>A.464(12), November 19th, 1981</li><li>A.626(15), November 19th, 1987</li><li>A.678(16), October 19th, 1989</li><li>A.736(18),November 4th, 1993</li><li>A.910(22), November 29th, 2001</li><li>A.1004(25), November 29th, 2007</li><li>A.1085(28), December 4th, 2013</li></ul></li></ul>	<ul><li>Inland Navigational Rules Act of 1980, see 94 stat. 3415, 33 CFR 83</li><li>Amendments to the Inland Navigation Rules (33 CFR 83); Federal Register documents:<ul><li>79 FR 37898, July 2nd, 2014</li><li>79 FR 68619, November 18th, 2014</li><li>80 FR 44274, July 27th, 2015</li><li>82 FR 35073, July 18th, 2017</li><li>83 FR 3273, January 24th, 2018</li><li>84 FR 30870, June 28th, 2019</li></ul></li></ul>

Navigation Rules 1999-2013 compilation of changes, compilation with reference sources, 33 CFR 83-88 redline version. For additional U.S. navigation regulations see Title 33 of the U.S. Code and U.S. Code of Federal Regulations.

***

www.ingramcontent.com/pod-product-compliance
Lightning Source LLC
Chambersburg PA
CBHW050620110426
42813CB00010B/2627